CW01648307

The Psychology of Information Security

Resolving conflicts between security compliance and human behaviour

Second edition

The Psychology of Information Security

Resolving conflicts between security compliance and human behaviour

Second edition

LERON ZINATULLIN

GRC Solutions

Every possible effort has been made to ensure that the information in this book is accurate at the time of going to press, and the publisher and the author cannot accept responsibility for any errors or omissions however caused. Any opinions expressed in this book are those of the author, not the publisher, and are in no way reflective of the author's employer, nor is it affiliated with the author's employer in any way. Websites identified are for reference only, not endorsement, and any website visits are at the reader's own risk. No responsibility for loss or damage occasioned to any person acting, or refraining from action, as a result of the material in this publication can be accepted by the publisher or the author.

Apart from any fair dealing for the purposes of research or private study, or criticism or review, as permitted under the Copyright, Designs and Patents Act 1988, this publication may only be reproduced, stored or transmitted, in any form, or by any means, with the prior permission in writing of the publisher or, in the case of reprographic reproduction, in accordance with the terms of licences issued by the Copyright Licensing Agency. Enquiries concerning reproduction outside those terms should be sent to the publishers at the following address:

GRC Solutions
Unit 3, Clive Court Bartholomew's Walk
Cambridgeshire Business Park
Ely, Cambridgeshire
CB7 4EA
United Kingdom
www.itgovernance.co.uk

© Leron Zinatullin 2016, 2026

The author has asserted the rights of the author under the Copyright, Designs and Patents Act, 1988, to be identified as the author of this work.

First published in the United Kingdom in 2016 by IT Governance Publishing:
ISBN 978-1-84928-789-0

Second edition published in the United Kingdom by GRC Solutions:
ISBN 978-1-78778-609-7

INTRODUCTION TO THE SECOND EDITION

A lot has changed since this book was published in 2016.

The book was updated to match the modern environment and incorporate new developments and research. Some content was removed – nobody has the time to read a long book!

The security industry has continued to mature, with new laws and regulations driving the evolution globally.

The most dramatic change, however, was the wide adoption of artificial intelligence (AI).

Adversaries' use of AI to increase efficiency, speed up attacks, lower their costs and mitigate the challenges of attracting skilled staff in an already constrained environment emerged as a concerning trend.

Social engineering remains one of the most prevalent attack vectors. Historically, crafting a believable phishing email required significant labour: days, sometimes weeks of research. Now, AI accelerates the process, allowing attackers to analyse large datasets, prioritise victims and even adjust ransom demands based on a victim's profile.

The use of AI for deep fake videos and voice impersonations is making social engineering attacks much more dangerous.

AI is used for defence too. By adopting more adaptive approaches, organisations can tackle the human vulnerabilities that attackers exploit most. When done well, security doesn't just educate – it protects.

Although this book is not about AI, it advocates for a socio-technical methodology to mitigate cyber threats.

People-centred approaches can help develop personalised and contextualised solutions to address ethical, legal and social challenges – things that cannot be solved with AI automation alone. That's what this book is about.

Although a lot has changed since the first edition, many things are the same: people have biases, security controls get in the way of productivity, risk management is complex and security culture is hard to build. Above all, critical thinking, emotional intelligence, empathy, trust, communication and human connection remain vital.

That's not something AI can replace any time soon. Understanding the organisational context, deciphering behavioural change and mastering the human aspects of cyber to create value is something this book will help you excel at.

FOREWORD

So often, information security is viewed as a technical discipline – a world of firewalls, antivirus software, access controls and encryption; an opaque and enigmatic discipline that defies understanding, with a priesthood who often protect their profession with complex concepts, language and, most of all, secrecy.

Leron takes a practical, pragmatic and no-holds-barred approach to demystifying the topic. He reminds us that ultimately security depends on people, and that we all act in what we see as our rational self-interest – sometimes ill-informed, ill-judged, even downright perverse.

No approach to security can ever succeed without considering people. As a profession, we need to look beyond our computers to understand the business, the culture of the organisation, and, most of all, how we can create a security environment that helps people feel free to do their job.

David Ferbrache OBE, FBCS, FIET

Managing Director, Beyond Blue Limited

Former Head of Cyber & Space, UK Ministry of Defence | Global Head of Cyber Futures, KPMG

Author of *A Pathology of Computer Viruses* and *Unix Installation Security and Integrity*

PREFACE

Mr Johnston was responsible for safety at an engineering company.[1] Among other duties, he had to ensure that employees were wearing their hard hats while on the job. His common strategy was to spot people who didn't follow this policy, approach them, quote the regulation and insist on compliance. He succeeded in having them abide by the rules, but only temporarily: employees usually removed their hats as soon as he left.

He decided to try something different. Instead of speaking to workers with authority, he became genuinely interested in why they didn't wear the hats, such as if the hats were uncomfortable.

Also, rather than simply insisting that employees follow the policy, he explained that it was important to wear hard hats because they were designed to prevent injuries and this was in workers' best interest. As a result, this not only increased compliance but also mitigated resentment towards the regulation.

Security professionals face a similar problem. They must ensure that an organisation is adequately addressing cyber security risks, but they also have to communicate the value of security appropriately to be successful.

On the one hand, not putting security controls in place may result in significant losses for an organisation. On the other, badly implemented security mechanisms may obstruct

---

[1] Carnegie, D., 2019, How to Win Friends and Influence People, Jaico Publishing House.

employees' productivity and result in a poor security culture.

The main goal of this book is to provide a set of recommendations to support the security professional's decision-making when designing and implementing security mechanisms, driving behavioural change, and embedding these changes across an organisation.

The book draws on the experience of industry experts and cross-disciplinary research to find the balance between security and productivity and build a positive culture of security.

ABOUT THE AUTHOR

Leron is a forward-thinking technology leader specialising in cyber security strategy, management and delivery. He has led large-scale, global, high-value security transformation projects to improve cost performance and support business strategy.

Leron has extensive knowledge and practical experience in solving information security, privacy and architectural issues across private and public sectors. His business acumen, technology insight and leadership allow him to enable organisations to grow and innovate while protecting them against cyber threats.

He has an MBA from the University of New South Wales and an MSc in Information Security from University College London, where he focused on the human aspects of information security. His research was related to modelling conflicts between security compliance and human behaviour and combating scams using AI.

Leron is an ethical leadership award recipient and recognised as one of the top cyber security leaders driving innovation and demonstrating value.

Website: *zinatullin.com*

ACKNOWLEDGEMENTS

I would like to thank the many people who helped me with this book: those who provided support, talked things over, offered comments and assisted in the editing.

CONTENTS

CHAPTER 1: MASTERING THE HUMAN FACTOR

Excelling in security means mastering the human factors: how people think, decide and act under real-world pressures. By applying behavioural science, security professionals can design systems that work with human nature instead of against it.

A socio-technical approach recognises that technology and human behaviour are inseparable: every control is shaped by the environment in which it operates. When security is built to fit how people work, it stops being an obstacle and becomes a core part of the organisation.

Security professionals must show how protective measures help the organisation achieve its mission and thrive in the face of cyber threats, by enabling innovation and improving resilience. This means framing security in terms of business objectives and people's needs. Security professionals should study the organisation's goals and articulate how better security supports them, demonstrating that risk reduction and stability foster growth and creativity.[2]

When everyone sees security as helping them do their job safely and confidently, rather than as a hurdle, it becomes part of the normal workflow instead of an 'extra' task. At the same time, security professionals must recognise and manage goal conflicts: situations where fast execution and security pull in different directions. In practice, people will

---

[2] Government Security Group, 2024, 'Improving security culture', UK Government.

typically do what they must to satisfy customers and deadlines, even if that means bending the rules. A mature culture treats these conflicts as systemic design issues, not personal failures.

Security mechanisms should be designed so that 'secure by default' is the norm, where updates and checks happen without disrupting work. When friction arises, teams work together to find fixes so that secure practices are also efficient.

By aligning security tasks with how people work, and by giving people room to flag problems without blame, security professionals turn potential conflicts into opportunities for smarter policies and better controls.

A culture of security depends on trust. Security professionals must engage candidly with employees so that the latter report problems and suggest improvements. If people fear punishment for mistakes or omissions, they will hide issues instead of helping to solve them.

Security professionals can't overlook true malice, but they must be fair, transparent and consistent. That means explaining why rules exist, showing that policies are applied evenly and owning up to any security team missteps. When security professionals acknowledge their own errors and fix them openly, it builds a powerful sense of shared responsibility.

This mutual accountability fosters a psychologically safe environment: people feel free to ask questions, admit errors and speak up without fear of unfair blame.

In a safe climate, innovation and learning flourish. Staff will challenge processes constructively and bring ideas for improvement.

Critically, safety and trust must be modelled from the top down. Business leaders and security professionals alike should openly encourage the right behaviours, like asking for help and reporting incidents, and avoid shaming anyone for honest mistakes.

By celebrating when employees do 'the right thing' and by responding to incidents as learning moments, security professionals help create a positive culture where everyone takes ownership of security.

When a vulnerability is exposed, security professionals should help quickly fix the gap and update their approach; in doing so, the organisation becomes more resilient and prepared for the next threat.

This requires an iterative approach: plan carefully, implement changes, measure the results, learn and repeat. Security professionals should continually gather feedback from employees, analyse near-misses and refine policies and security mechanisms accordingly.

Encouraging this agility means security professionals must stay in close contact with all parts of the business. When new technology or business needs arise, security professionals should work with stakeholders to adapt security mechanisms proactively. By remaining open to change and quickly integrating lessons learned, security professionals embed resilience in the organisation. Staff see that security is evolving with them – not rigidly clinging to old rules – which builds confidence and engagement.

Security habits must be woven into the organisation's social fabric. When safe behaviours (like regular backups, software updates or reporting suspicious emails) become 'how we do things here', everyone is more likely to follow them.

Security professionals should ensure that good habits are visible and celebrated, such as highlighting that a team consistently applies a safe practice. This social reinforcement helps turn security from a checklist of dos and don'ts into a shared set of norms.

Regular communication, peer support and role-modelling are key. One practical approach is to build security champion networks: representatives in each department or team who understand both the local work context and the security goals. These champions act as a bridge between the security team and the rest of the organisation, spreading knowledge in ways tailored to each group's needs.

Champions can gather feedback on what is and isn't working, and suggest improvements that make sense on the ground. In effect, they help make secure actions not just required, but also relatable and routine. Over time, this grassroots reinforcement makes secure behaviour feel as ordinary as any other core value.

Culture flows from the top. Every leader – from the boardroom to frontline supervisors – must visibly support and embody the security vision. Leaders shape norms by their own actions: if a department head follows security protocols and encourages team members to do so, others will follow suit.

Conversely, if a manager flouts rules (for example, by using unauthorised devices or skipping compulsory training), people will learn that security is optional. Effective security leadership means actively championing the vision and goals. Leaders should communicate clear security objectives to their teams and tie them to the broader mission. They need to understand the realities of how people work (and what pressures they face) so that they can advocate for security initiatives that fit into day-to-day workflows. By doing so, leaders take responsibility for their impact on culture and signal to everyone that security is a priority worthy of investment.

Every employee needs the tools and knowledge to contribute to security. Policies must be clear, accessible and up to date – neither so complex that people give up on them, nor so vague that nobody knows what is expected.

The right balance means writing rules in plain language, making them easy to find and continually updating them as technology and threats change. It also means providing real-world context and examples so people understand why a policy matters to their work.

Education campaigns should reinforce that every person's behaviour matters. Security professionals should stress that reporting incidents and following policies do make a difference.

Feedback loops are essential. Security professionals must measure engagement (surveys, metrics) and use that data to refine their training approach and policies.

Building a resilient security culture requires sustained effort, clear leadership and collaboration across the organisation. Security professionals should continually measure and monitor their progress – but focus on meaningful results, not vanity metrics. For example, track whether employees feel confident in handling security tasks, whether they believe their actions matter and how promptly issues get reported.[3]

A strong culture of security means everyone – from executives to new hires – understands that they share the responsibility and benefit of staying secure. By framing security as integral to success, fostering trust and openness, adapting through learning, reinforcing good norms, leading by example and providing clear support, security professionals create a vigilant, resilient community of defenders. This collaborative environment makes security second nature. With leaders championing the way and people confident in their role, security becomes a true enabler of the organisation's mission, today and in the challenges of tomorrow.

---

[3] National Cyber Security Centre, 2025, 'Cyber security culture principles'.

CHAPTER 2: THE FOUNDATION OF INFORMATION SECURITY AND RISK

Security controls don't operate in isolation – they must align seamlessly with the people who use them. As threats evolve, organisations rely on engaged employees ready to take an active role in protecting the company. Yet fostering secure behaviour is a continuous journey without a quick fix.

Rather than blaming staff as the 'weakest link' when breaches occur, security professionals can leverage employees' existing knowledge and skills to strengthen the organisation's defences.

Organisations rely on staff who feel empowered and ready to confront novel cyber threats. Under the right circumstances, people can perform 'heroic' actions[4]: creative, effective responses to new attacks that slip past standard defences.

Such acts of security heroism depend on people who are genuinely invested in their work and backed by the trust and support of their organisation.

To achieve this and improve the security culture, it's important to build on solid foundations. These foundations start with understanding the fundamentals of information security, risk management and communication.

---

[4] Reason, J., 2017, The Human Contribution: Unsafe Acts, Accidents and Heroic Recoveries, CRC Press.

Information security issues in organisations were being raised long before the rapid development of technology. Companies have always been concerned with protecting their confidential information, including their intellectual property and trade secrets. In other words, all organisations have assets, which help them deliver value to stakeholders, for example generate revenue. The goal of information security is to identify and protect these assets.

Engaging business stakeholders can help identify the assets for which confidentiality, integrity and availability is a critical requirement. The organisation defines what needs to be protected, and security professionals help determine appropriate protection measures.

It is here that security professionals face their first challenge: the language of the organisation and the language of information security are different, and it is their responsibility to manage this translation effectively.

Thankfully, business and security professionals have a common ground: they are both involved in managing risk.

***

Risk is "the effect of uncertainty on objectives".[5]

The people, processes and technology supporting the organisation's objectives are not bulletproof, and their

---

[5] International Organization for Standardization, (2020) 'ISO 31000 Risk management', Geneva.

weaknesses may be exploited. A scenario in which a threat actor exploits such a weakness can vary in likelihood and impact on company assets.

For example, in an organisation that handles customers' personal data online, the probability of human error leading to disclosure of sensitive information may be greater and have a more significant business impact than someone bringing down the website.

Likewise, the exploitation of a vulnerable critical business system may have a greater impact than that of one used solely for non-essential administrative services.

This relationship between likelihood and impact is at the core of risk management.

To reduce the probability (and sometimes the impact) of the threat, security professionals can implement countermeasures, or security controls.

When thinking in terms of protection measures, it is useful to know who the attackers are. Security professionals should understand that attackers differ in resources, motivation, ability and risk propensity.

There are various techniques to help with threat modelling. In general terms, however, it can be helpful to define specific threat actors and their target, motivation and impact on the organisation. Table 1 can be used as a starting point to define your own:

Table 1: Example threat actors

Threat actor	Description	Motivation(s)	Target(s)	Impact on organisation
Organised crime	International hacking groups	Financial gain	Commercial data, personal data for identity fraud	Reputational damage, regulatory fines, loss of customer trust
Insider	Intentional or unintentional	Human error, grudge, financial gain	Intellectual property, commercial data	Destruction or alteration of information, theft of information, reputational damage, regulatory fines
Competitors	Espionage and sabotage	Competitive advantage	Intellectual property, commercial information	Disruption or destruction, theft of information, reputational damage, loss of customers
State-sponsored	Espionage	Political	Intellectual property, commercial data, personal data	Theft of information, reputational damage

Security professionals can use their understanding of assets and threats relevant to their organisation to identify security risks. For instance:

- Breach of sensitive data: regulatory fines, potential litigation and loss of customer trust due to accidental mishandling, external system compromise or insider threat leading to exposure of sensitive data.
- Failure to comply with relevant regulations: revenue loss and reputational damage due to fines and unwanted media attention because of non-compliance with the GDPR, the PCI DSS, etc.

- Disruption of operations: decreased productivity or inability to trade due to compromise of IT systems by malicious actor, denial-of-service attacks, sabotage or employee error.

These high-level risks should be tailored to the context of the organisation. It's also worth remembering that this is not a one-off exercise. Tracking assets, threats and risks should be part of the security management function and be incorporated into operational risk management and continual improvement cycles.

Furthermore, not every downside risk should be eliminated. Information security should support and enable the organisation. As such, security professionals must consider the cost of implementing countermeasures. They should implement the controls ensuring that the cost is appropriate for the asset to which it is applied.

Often perceived negatively, operational risk-taking is required to realise business opportunities. Security professionals, therefore, may benefit from also communicating information security risks to the organisation in a positive way.

For example, employees may believe that security professionals' only priority is to stop malware on their devices to prevent widespread infection across the network. However, there is also a direct productivity benefit. Malware prevention can increase the availability of resources and the efficiency of employees, because people can focus on their work rather than waiting for their laptop to be cleared or rebuilt.

Threats in this paradigm could be replaced by opportunities, vulnerabilities by strengths, and impact by benefits.

Business stakeholders care about maximising opportunities, enhancing brand reputation and building customer trust. Security professionals can support these but must first establish what the organisation's priorities are. To do this, they must engage people to understand the organisation's drivers, goals and objectives.

A clear link should be preserved between business concerns and security countermeasures so that security professionals can demonstrate the value they bring.

CHAPTER 3: UNDERSTANDING THE RISK CONTEXT

Organisational strategy and risk are intertwined. Any decision concerning strategy will have risk considerations.

In the world of financial crises, climate change, pandemics and geopolitical instability, risk is everywhere. Therefore, it's helpful to adopt a structured way of analysing it.

PESTLE is a framework that helps 'scan' the external macro environment for factors that may impact the performance of the organisation. This framework groups these external factors into six categories: Political, Economic, Sociocultural, Technological, Legal (Regulatory) and Environmental as shown in Table 2.

Table 2: PESTLE analysis

Category	Description	Examples
Political	Factors that are driven by government policies and regulation	Competition regulations, taxation, government spending and stimulus
Economic	Factors that are related to the economy	Interest rates, employment rates, exchange rates, inflation rates
Sociocultural	Factors that are related to	Demographics, attitudes and

	societal values, lifestyle and beliefs	consumer concerns
Technological	Factors related to technological development and pace of change in technology	Automation, robotics, artificial intelligence, genetic engineering
Legal	Factors in the regulatory environment and changes expected in regulations	Cyber security and data protection regulation, intellectual property law, corporate law, employment law, industry-specific regulation
Environmental	Factors that are related to the environment	Extreme weather events, climate change

The PESTLE analysis uncovers both threats to realising the business objectives and opportunities for an organisation in pursuit of its strategy.

The PESTLE framework enables security professionals to see the bigger picture of enterprise-wide risks. This, in turn, encourages early identification of risk treatment options in a proactive manner.

Security professionals should start by assessing the relevance of each category to the given industry and organisational context, identify the data points for each applicable category, and draw conclusions from the analysis.

Insights should be converted into action plans to exploit opportunities and mitigate threats. These can be captured in another widely used business tool: SWOT.

SWOT stands for Strengths, Weaknesses, Opportunities and Threats. This simple technique involves listing external and internal factors that are helpful and harmful for an organisation.

	Helpful	**Harmful**
Internal	Strengths	Weaknesses
External	Opportunities	Threats

Figure 1: SWOT analysis

This framework builds on the external PESTLE analysis and introduces factors internal to the organisation: strengths and weaknesses.

The dynamic interplay between these factors can help inform the strategy. Weaknesses that may be exploited by threats should be mitigated, where possible. For instance, in the security context, adopting a vulnerability management programme aims to counter the external threat of a weakness being exploited by external attackers.

Robust security controls themselves can be viewed as a strength. They can help the organisation take advantage of a business opportunity by increasing customer trust: a business partner could be reassured as to the safety of doing business with a company if this organisation had implemented adequate security measures.

If security professionals can connect the benefits of a security programme to the ability of an organisation to increase sales, to launch new digital products, to safely enter riskier markets, to give assurance to its clients and to bring confidence to the industry, then they are adding value to the business. If security professionals are just doing security for security's sake, they may be inadvertently stifling the organisation rather than supporting it.

The foundation of an effective strategy is understanding both the external and internal environments.

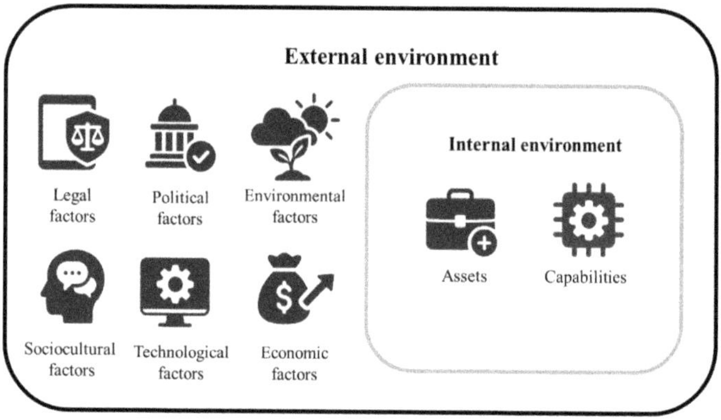

Figure 2: External and internal factors

The first step in supporting the organisation is to understand it. Mission, purpose and values drive the strategy.

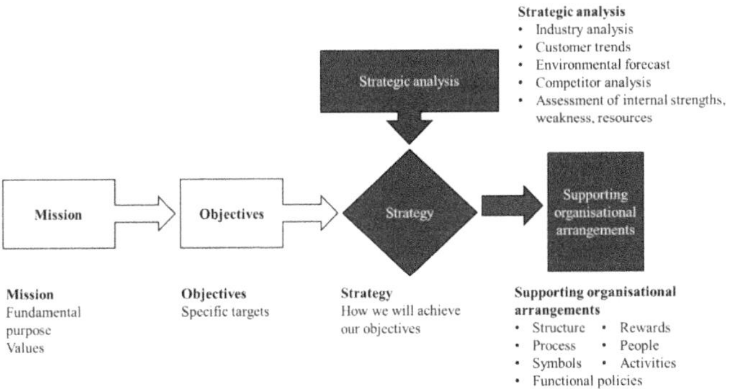

Figure 3: Mission-objectives-strategy framework[6]

Vision is a forward-looking statement of what the organisation is aiming to achieve. *Mission* outlines what the organisation does, while *values* indicate what it believes in. Lastly, *objectives* define specific performance outcomes.

Security professionals should tailor their security programmes to organisational objectives and business risks.

Many organisations publish an annual report with a section on business risks. It's a good starting point to align security risks to these to speak the same language.

Remember: doing business means taking risks. Therefore, an organisation's risk appetite should be considered.

---

[6] Adapted from Hambrick, D.C. and Fredrickson, J.W., 2001. 'Are you sure you have a strategy?', Academy of Management Perspectives, 15(4), pp.48-59.

Risk appetite is the "amount and type of risk that an organisation is willing to pursue or retain".[7] In other words, it's the level of risk exposure that the organisation is willing to accept within its capacity to achieve its strategic objectives.

Different risk appetite levels can be in place for each key risk area: it can be low for health and safety or financial compliance but high for innovation or new ventures.

As risk appetite is usually set by the board, it is perfectly normal to retain a risk that falls below this threshold, even if this is viewed differently by the security professional. The board's role is to optimise the risk position, not minimise it – some risks are actively pursued to generate value for stakeholders.

---

[7] International Organization for Standardization (ISO), 2009, 'ISO Guide 73:2009 Risk management - Vocabulary.' Geneva.

CHAPTER 4: THE PSYCHOLOGY OF RISK MANAGEMENT

Risk management goes beyond understanding the organisation and treating risk; it has a psychological aspect that is often overlooked. People perceive risk differently, and this affects their behaviour.

Faced with uncertainty, people protect perceived gains and, at the same time, are willing to take extra risk to recover perceived losses.[8]

To demonstrate the complexity of decision-making, researchers gave participants £1,000 and asked if they would prefer to give £500 back and keep the remaining £500, or flip a coin to win the full amount for heads or lose the full amount for tails.

Most participants chose the safe option of receiving a guaranteed £500.

In the second scenario, participants were given £2,000 and were presented with a similar choice. This time, they could choose to either give £500 back or flip a coin where they could lose £1,000 or win the entire pot.

Most participants chose the second option.

This demonstrates that there are different psychological associations with gains and losses. This makes it more

---

[8] Kahneman, D. and Tversky, A., 1979, 'Prospect theory: an analysis of decision under risk', Econometrica, 47(2), pp. 263–291.

difficult for a security professional to communicate the value of security to business stakeholders.

Asymmetric perception of gains and losses is not the only reason for the additional complexity of decision-making. The perception of risk can also be clouded by people's experiences and expectations.

Security professionals must navigate both scientifically grounded risks and 'virtual' risks – those areas where evidence is unclear and people fall back on their beliefs, convictions, prejudices or superstitions.[9]

People vary in their propensity to take risks, which is influenced by their perception, the potential reward and their experience of loss.

If someone experienced a negative event in the past, they assign a disproportionately high probability and impact to that situation compared to an unknown event, even if probability theory tells us otherwise.

On the other hand, people tend to overestimate spectacular but rare risks, but downplay common risks, which can be as harmful for the organisation, if not more so.

Risk management plans do not guarantee success and may result in a false sense of safety, increasing risk.[10] Security professionals may observe similar convictions in their organisations: "we have a firewall, so we must be secure".

---

[9] Adams, J., 2007 'Risk management: It's not rocket science… it's much more complicated', Risk Management, 54(5), pp. 36–40.

[10] Klein, G., 2009, Streetlights and shadows: searching for the keys to adaptive decision making, MIT Press.

The complexities of human behaviour as it relates to risk management are compounded by additional complexities of risk identification. This is illustrated by the concept of black swan events,[11] where some occurrences cannot be predicted, even with unlimited resources.

Before the discovery of the Australian continent, scientists believed that, following years of observation, all swans were white. In their limited realm of experience, they did not consider that there could be any other type of swan. Therefore, when explorers encountered the black swan species variation in Australia, it was an unexpected, unpredictable event. This demonstrates that empirical evidence is not sufficient to confidently predict the absence of outliers.

Consider Mirage Casino's four largest losses.[12] These comprised an unsuccessful attempt to bomb the casino, a ransom demand for the owner's kidnapped daughter, a fine due to negligence in completing tax returns, and a tiger mauling.

How many of these risks could have been foreseen and managed appropriately, preventing such losses in the first place?

Instead of assessing those risks with low probability and high impact, casinos tend to focus on high-probability, low-impact events, such as preventing cheating at the tables.

---

[11] Taleb, N. N., 2010, The black swan: the impact of the highly improbable fragility, Vol. 2, Random House.

[12] Ibid.

Thorough risk assessment and identification is not the only challenge; there may also be unforeseen consequences of taking action to address risks.

Let's consider an example where the manager of a nightclub is concerned about the recent diminishing revenue. He regularly observes many people inside the club, but the profits from the entrance fees are lower than expected.

The manager initially suspects that employee fraud is to blame; however, after investigating, it turns out that only a few customers were entering via the front door and paying for their ticket. As soon as they got in, they let their friends in through the fire escape.

He therefore may choose to prevent this behaviour by jamming the fire exit doors shut, without considering the increased risk to health and safety for his employees and guests as a direct result of his actions.

This may lead to a tragedy and subsequent loss of life in the event of a fire.

Accountability for risk should be delegated to an individual with authority and resources to manage the risk.

A CFO, for instance, may be interested in maximising profits, regardless of compliance. A head of compliance, on the other hand, is concerned with potential fines for violating regulations. They can escalate the risk to the CEO, whose responsibility it is to decide on which action to take.

Such an approach demonstrates that identification of risks is not enough: each risk should have a person who is accountable for it. If the organisation believes that security professionals are responsible for closing the doors, they will leave them open.

Everything that has been discussed so far makes the job of a security professional much more challenging. After all, "risk management is not rocket science – it's much more complicated."[13]

Good risk management, therefore, requires good decision-making.

---

[13] Adams, J., 2007, 'Risk Management: It's Not Rocket Science ... It's Much More Complicated', Risk Management, 54(5), pp.36–41.

CHAPTER 5: THE PSYCHOLOGY OF DECISION-MAKING

Decisions come from both thinking and feeling – although sometimes our emotions take over completely. Paul MacLean's triune brain model[14] helps explain decision-making.

He divided the brain into three parts. The oldest part, the brainstem, handles basic survival: heartbeat, breathing, reproduction and defence. Next is the limbic system, where memories and emotions live; it includes the amygdala, which triggers fear. The newest part, the neocortex, lets us think and reason.

MacLean's model shows that emotions and logic work in different brain areas. Emotions push us to act quickly – fighting or fleeing – while reasoning guides those impulses. Emotions don't wait for us to think things through; they make us move.

Emotions are vital for making decisions – if people damage the emotional centres, they struggle to decide at all. But unrecognised biases can twist our feelings and weaken decisions. The aim is not to remove emotion. Instead, good decision makers learn to spot when feelings might cloud their judgement and develop the emotional know-how to keep them in check.

---

[14] MacLean, P.D., 1990, The Triune Brain in Evolution: Role in Paleocerebral Functions, Springer Science & Business Media.

There are four *emotional tags*[15] that can sway decisions:

1. Strong past experiences: Powerful memories of success, failure or fear can dominate our choices.
2. Fixed judgements: Even helpful beliefs can lock us into thinking that no longer fits.
3. Personal interests: If our own benefit clashes with wider needs, we can lose perspective.
4. Attachments: Bonds with people, places or things can induce bias when those ties are at stake.

Recognising these emotional tags can help security professionals handle conflicts of interest, appreciate how feelings affect choices, and blend emotion and reason to make better decisions.

***

Decisions often start with a 'gut feeling'. Where does this intuition come from? Pure instinct, a snap judgement without any reasoning, or something else entirely?

It can be examined using two systems in the brain[16]:

---

[15] Finkelstein, S., Whitehead, J. and Campbell, A., 2008, Think Again: Why Good Leaders Make Bad Decisions and How to Keep it From Happening to You, Harvard Business Press, Boston.
[16] Kahneman, D., 2011, Thinking, Fast and Slow, Penguin Books, London.

- System 1 operates automatically and quickly. It uses mental shortcuts (heuristics) and is prone to biases.
- System 2 works slowly and deliberately. It evaluates information carefully and applies logic.

Contrary to our self-perception, System 1 does most of the heavy lifting. It generates impressions and feelings almost instantly. System 2 then builds on those to form our conscious judgements.

Most everyday actions (clicking links, logging into sites) happen under System 1, causing people to rely on mental shortcuts when assessing risks. Threat actors increasingly exploit these heuristics in social engineering attacks.

To combat this, most anti-phishing efforts train staff to 'think before you click', engaging System 2. But requiring people to pause and analyse every link imposes a heavy cognitive load[17] and detracts from their primary tasks – something we will explore in Chapter 11.

A better strategy is to block or filter out as many phishing attempts as possible before they arrive, then equip employees with a simple reporting and feedback system so they can quickly verify suspicious emails (Chapter 13). Additionally, educating staff about common manipulation tactics, such as appeals to authority or urgency (Chapter 7), enables them to recognise a broader range of social engineering techniques without slowing their day-to-day work.

---

[17] The European Union Agency for Cybersecurity (ENISA), 2018, 'Cybersecurity Culture Guidelines: Behavioural Aspects of Cybersecurity'.

Decision-making must be seen in the context of learning: people form expectations from experience and adjust based on feedback.[18] In security, this means that people learn over time which behaviours are safe.

Repeated experiences train System 1 so well that it can produce accurate intuitions before System 2 has time to think things through. That's why an experienced doctor can often diagnose a patient at a glance, or a judge might immediately sense whether a witness is honest. It also means people can get better at spotting scams.

Despite its power, intuition can be risky because our biases can lead us astray. There are two conditions for trusting an expert's gut judgement[19]:

1. A regular environment, where patterns repeat and are predictable.
2. Extensive practice, so the expert has learned those patterns deeply.

For security professionals, it's important to know when you're relying on intuition and to test that instinct against other perspectives, data and analyses. Of course, be aware of the common biases and traps that can derail good decision-making.

---

[18] Newell, B.R., Lagnado, D.A. and Shanks, D.R., 2022. Straight Choices: The Psychology of Decision Making, Psychology Press.

[19] Kahneman, D., 2011, Thinking, Fast and Slow, Penguin Books, London.

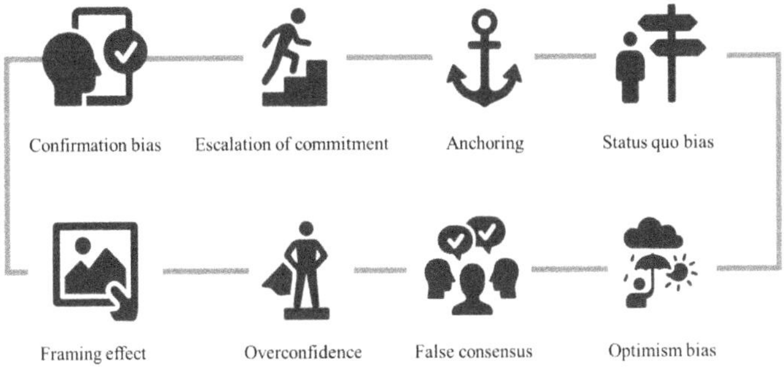

Figure 4: Most common biases

The most common individual decision biases are[20]:

- Confirmation bias: Looking for information that supports what you already believe and ignoring anything that contradicts it. For example, focusing only on why a security project will succeed and downplaying reasons it might fail.
- Escalation of commitment (sunk-cost fallacy): Sticking with a decision because you've invested time or money. For instance, after spending heavily on a new security solution, security professionals may keep throwing money at it to justify the original outlay even if proven ineffective.
- Anchoring: Relying too heavily on the first number or piece of information you hear. For example, if an early cost estimate for a project is £50 million, later estimates might all seem low or high compared to

[20] Hammond, J.S., Keeney, R.L. and Raiffa, H., 2006, 'The Hidden Traps in Decision Making', Harvard Business Review.

that initial figure – even if the first was just a rough guess.

- Status-quo bias: Preferring things to stay the same. Faced with a new cyber risk, people may procrastinate or choose the 'least-bad' option rather than addressing it.
- Framing effect: Letting the way a problem is presented shape your choice. Describing a new security mechanism as an opportunity to build trust with customers will lead to different solutions than calling it a compliance obligation.
- Overconfidence: Being too sure of your own abilities and overly optimistic about outcomes. In a group that only shares 'good news', security professionals may become complacent, believing 'we're fine' even when warning signs are there, overestimating security readiness.
- False consensus: Going along with the loudest voices in a group because quieter people give up or feel they have no choice.
- Optimism bias: Overestimating good results and underestimating costs or challenges. Research[21] shows that most big projects run late and over budget, and many mergers and market entries fail to live up to expectations, often because planners overlook risks and stick to 'best-case' scenarios.

[21] Lovallo, D and Kahneman, D., 2003, 'Delusions of Success: How Optimism Undermines Executives' Decisions', Harvard Business Review.

Another example is the belief that data breaches are not going to happen to them.

The more security professionals understand their own biases, the better they can spot and correct them. Security professionals should keep these traps in mind, deliberately slow down when needed, and build checks – like asking for alternative views or running 'what-if' scenarios – to catch biased thinking before it leads to poor decisions.

These cognitive distortions are not fixed. Security professionals can adopt a growth mindset to overcome them. Growth mindset is the belief that performance is shaped more by effort, learning and strategy than by fixed traits such as intelligence or background.[22]

Rather than seeing ability as something innate and unchangeable, a growth mindset assumes that skills and behaviours can be developed through persistence and deliberate practice. This perspective encourages self-reflection, resilience and continual improvement, reinforcing the idea that one's capabilities are within one's own control.

The more security professionals understand their own drivers and behaviour, the better they'll be at seeing what motivates others.

Deep self-reflection matters because it shapes how people judge, decide and behave.

---

[22] Dweck, C.S., 2006, Mindset: The New Psychology of Success, Random House.

There are four stages of self-reflection[23]:

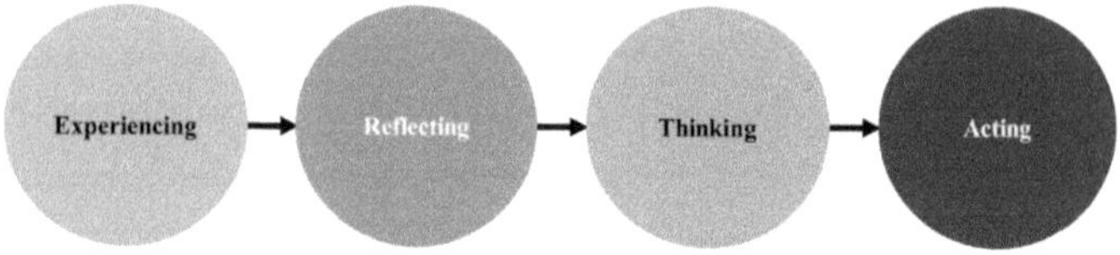

Figure 5: Self-reflection

1. Experiencing: living through an event or a situation.
2. Reflecting: pausing afterwards to notice thoughts and feelings.
3. Thinking: making sense of what happened and why.
4. Acting: applying what you've learned the next time around.

All four steps are needed for real growth.

Bringing in diverse perspectives is another way to improve decision-making.

A study of top-performing forecasting teams[24] identified the common thread in their decision-making: "diversity trumps ability". Teams of highly intelligent individuals with similar backgrounds were outdone by groups of less brilliant but more varied members. What truly mattered

[23] Kolb and Kolb quoted in E Anderson and J Neild, 2007, 'Improving self-reflection and peer feedback', Department of Management Working Paper Series, Working Paper 14/07.
[24] Tetlock, P.E. and Gardner, D., 2016, Superforecasting: The Art and Science of Prediction, Random House.

wasn't raw intellect but open-mindedness and a culture that encouraged sharing.

Group decision-making excels because it brings together different viewpoints and methods, promoting idea generation and innovation. In practice, the greater the diversity, the richer the pool of alternatives and insights available to guide choices.

People naturally favour their own viewpoint, often rating it above others due to self-serving bias. Such biases can hamper both interpersonal dynamics and group discussions, and stifle attention to alternative ideas.

To leverage people's diverse viewpoints, security professionals must carve out space to surface and genuinely consider each perspective. Though challenging, this openness can yield deeper understanding and more refined, well-informed decisions.

For routine decisions, homogeneity may suffice, but security professionals often grapple with high-stakes, complex, multifaceted issues that demand a broad range of insights.

They appreciate diversity because they know no single individual – no matter how capable – can encompass every angle needed for optimal decisions.

To unlock true collective intelligence, team members must cultivate self-awareness: understanding their own perceptual strengths ("What unique perspective do I bring?") and valuing those of their colleagues ("What do they contribute?"), with the conviction that every viewpoint adds worth.

Getting better at decision-making isn't a one-and-done task. It requires a commitment to continual learning through deliberate practices like mentoring, honest feedback and regular self-reflection.

CHAPTER 6: THE PSYCHOLOGY OF COMMUNICATION

One of the most important, yet underappreciated, skills for security professionals is active listening.

Despite common belief, it doesn't only involve reiterating messages and asking follow-up questions. It happens on a deeper level.

When listening actively, you try to understand the real problem by not jumping to conclusions or proposing a solution too soon. Listening in this manner expends a great deal of mental effort, and prevents tunnel vision around our own assumptions and stereotypes we discussed in the previous chapter.

One must be fully engaged in the present conversation, which requires minimising all external distractions, such as phone and emails, as well as making sure that the message is understood.

Word choices, tone of voice, gestures and facial expressions can be useful non-verbal cues. Research suggests that these factors carry much more meaning for humans than words.[25] This could be due to the evolution of our fight-or-flight decision-making processes, which have developed over millennia by reading body language.

---

[25] Mehrabian A. and Ferris, S.R., 'Inference of Attitudes from Nonverbal Communication in Two Channels', Journal of Consulting Psychology, 31(3), 1967, pp.248–252.

Active listening incorporates both verbal and non-verbal aspects of communication. This can help security professionals understand business stakeholders, which in turn would be valuable both in understanding existing challenges and in gaining the necessary support.

By paying attention, suspending judgement, and checking understanding, security professionals can become much stronger listeners – and communicators.

Communication can be viewed as a simple model, consisting of three parts: a sender, a receiver and a channel.

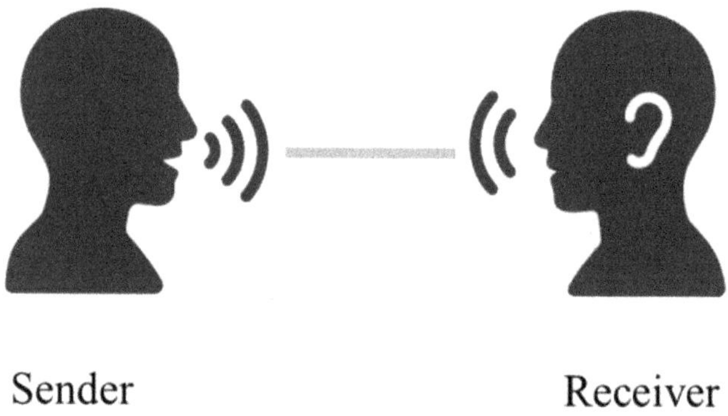

Figure 6: Simple communication model

Despite the simplicity of this model, many errors can occur. Their cause lies in the way we process and interpret information.

The sender 'encodes' the original message and relays it to the receiver. The resulting message may be different from what was intended, not only due to its dependency on the sender's communication skills but also because the receiver interprets the message based on their own values and experiences. The 'telephone' game played by children all over the world serves as a good illustration of this principle.

Our perception of information is based on the filters that we develop during childhood, which are formed as a result of our cultural and social background. Additionally, our brain, in an effort to process information in a more efficient manner, constantly omits and generalises our experiences, which can lead to miscommunication.

Security professionals should be aware of their assumptions and biases. Understanding past experiences and how they affect communication, emotions and the decision-making process is the foundation of emotional intelligence.

Emotional intelligence (often called EQ) refers to the ability to recognise, understand and manage our own emotions, as well as perceive and influence the feelings of others.[26]

For security professionals, whose roles often depend on guiding teams and shaping organisational culture, EQ is especially critical. Security professionals engage with many people, set the tone for their teams, and embody the organisation's values to both internal and external audiences. In other words, technical know-how might get

---

[26] Mayer, J.D., Caruso, D.R. and Salovey, P., 2016, 'The ability model of emotional intelligence: Principles and updates', Emotion Review, vol. 8, no. 4, pp.290–300.

you the job, but emotional intelligence is what helps you lead effectively once you're there.

Research[27] suggests that people with high emotional intelligence consistently outperform their peers. They do this by helping their teams stay composed when things go wrong (not an unusual event in cyber security), by fostering a positive atmosphere that encourages mutual support, and even by drawing top performers (for example as security champions) who want to work with leaders who understand and respect their feelings.

EQ becomes especially critical in security roles that demand emotional labour, where close collaboration is the norm and where decisions are reached by consensus rather than by issuing orders.[28] In these settings, the ability to read and manage emotions can make the difference between a stressed-out group and a high-performing team.[29]

---

[27] Miao, C., Humphrey, R.H. and Qian, S., 2018, 'A cross-cultural meta-analysis of how leader emotional intelligence influences subordinate task performance and organizational citizenship behavior', Journal of World Business, vol. 53, no. 4, pp.463–474.

[28] Walter, F., Cole, M.S. and Humphrey, R.H., 2011, 'Emotional Intelligence: Sine Qua Non of Leadership or Folderol?', Academy of Management Perspectives , vol. 25, no. 1, pp.45–59.

[29] MacCann, C., Joseph, D.L., Newman, D.A. and Roberts, R. D., 2014, 'Emotional intelligence is a second-stratum factor of intelligence: Evidence from hierarchical and bifactor models', Emotion, vol. 14, no. 2, pp.358–374.

Security professionals can use Goleman's framework[30] of EQ competencies to develop their EQ skills as shown in Table 3.

Table 3: Goleman's framework

Personal competence	Social competence
• Self-awareness Knowing one's internal states, preferences, resources and intuitions • Self-regulation Managing one's internal states, impulses and resources • Motivation Emotional tendencies that guide or facilitate reaching goals	• Empathy Awareness of other's feelings needs and concerns • Social skill Adeptness at inducing desirable responses in others

This framework offers security professionals a roadmap for better self-management and stronger relationships – both essential when defending complex systems under pressure.

Self-awareness in security hinges on emotional awareness (recognising when stress or frustration clouds your judgement), accurate self-assessment (being honest about where your technical strengths may outpace your people skills) and self-confidence (trusting your expertise to drive solutions).

---

[30] Goleman, D., 1998, Working with Emotional Intelligence, Bantam Books, New York; Goleman, D., Boyatzis, R. and A McKee, 2004, Primal Leadership: Learning to Lead With Emotional Intelligence, Harvard Business School Press, Boston.

Self-regulation means managing your emotions, impulses and energy. For instance, security professionals should resist panicking and locking out an entire user base at the first sign of unusual activity. Instead, they should calmly follow incident playbooks to isolate affected accounts, ensuring a measured response.

Motivation – our emotional drive – shows up when security professionals face a backlog of hundreds of critical vulnerabilities. Their achievement drive pushes them to prioritise and schedule fixes, commitment keeps cross-functional teams aligned, initiative sparks automation of testing workflows, and optimism – celebrating each reduction milestone – sustains momentum until risk is substantially lowered.

Empathy means tuning into others' feelings and concerns and adapting accordingly. For example, when a development team grows frustrated by lengthy security code reviews that stall sprint deadlines, security professionals pause to understand their workflow pressures. They then co-create a risk-based review process, automating scans to balance rapid release cycles with robust security and build trust across the organisation.

Finally, strong social skills let security professionals influence without authority: persuading executives to fund security initiatives by translating technical risk into potential financial impact.

Emotional intelligence and active listening are core components of effective communication. These are essential skills for security professionals who often need to navigate challenging stakeholder relationships. Doing so effectively allows security professionals to not only manage risk more effectively but also build the trust and collaboration critical for resilient, secure organisations.

CHAPTER 7: INFLUENCE AND TRUST

Key factors that underpin the success of a security function or initiative are:

- Integration. Security risk should be integrated into the overall organisational strategy and enterprise-wide risk management.
- Risk appetite. Business risk tolerance relative to security risk should be consistent with the strategy.
- Collaboration. Security professionals should collaborate with other stakeholders to ensure a systematic approach to security and the appropriate prioritisation of risk mitigation activities.

Building on the previous chapters and what we learned about strategy and risk management so far, let's turn our attention to collaboration.

Managing stakeholders gets increasingly complex in cross-functional engagements so common in the security field. The number of communication paths tends to increase dramatically with every new stakeholder introduced to the network.

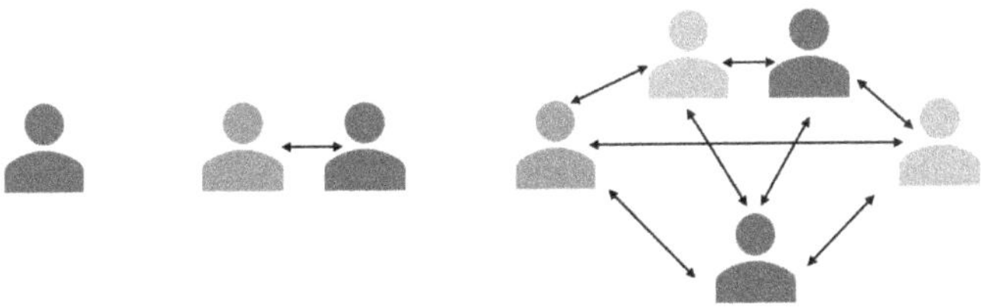

Figure 7: The complexity of communication

Stakeholder engagement is key in making sure that risks are addressed properly. The earlier people are involved in a security initiative, the easier it is to obtain their support. The same principle applies when security professionals are involved in other people's projects to provide guidance.

Security professionals first need to understand who the stakeholders are and how to keep them engaged.

A stakeholder in an organisation is any group or individual who can affect or is affected by the achievement of the organisation's objectives.[31]

Communicating new security policies, technology and practices to impacted teams is critical, especially in large organisations with many stakeholder groups spread across multiple geographies.

Stakeholders can be identified based on three variables: power, legitimacy and urgency.[32]

Urgency is "the degree to which stakeholder claims call for immediate attention". It is determined not only by time constraints but also by the significance of the relationship.

---

[31] R. Edward Freeman and John McVea, 'A Stakeholder Approach to Strategic Management', 2001.

[32] Mitchell, R. K, Agle, B. R and Wood, D.J., 'Toward a Theory of Stakeholder Identification and Salience: Defining the Principle of Who and What Really Counts', Academy of Management Review, 22(4), 1997, pp.853–886.

Power in this context is defined as the ability to influence decision-making in an organisation by material or social means.[33]

Legitimacy refers to those stakeholders who have a formal structure in place with which to affect the initiative or organisation. Examples of such stakeholders may include heads of departments, or those who sit on the board.

---

[33] Etzioni, A., Moral Dimension: Toward a New Economics, Simon and Schuster, 2010.

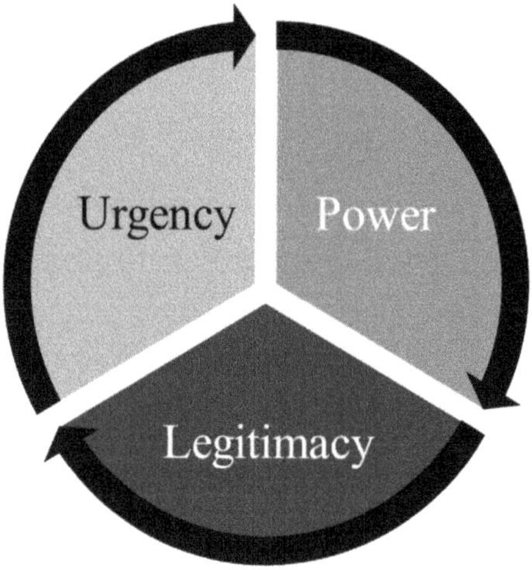

Figure 8: Stakeholder salience

Security professionals can prepare a communications plan to ensure that nobody is left out and stakeholders' interests are considered.

As a first step when devising the plan, a stakeholder register can be created that captures their contact information. It should also include the feedback received during the types of discussion with your stakeholders to understand their needs. Table 4 can help with capturing the expectations of the initiative, requirements and other insights.

Table 4: Stakeholder register

Name	Job title	Contact information	Expectation	Requirements	Influence	Comments

The "Influence" column is meant to contain relevant information regarding the power, legitimacy and urgency of the corresponding stakeholder. As with many other aspects of the security profession, extra care should be taken when handling this data.

As soon as the stakeholders are identified and their needs recorded, security professionals should engage them to understand their preferred method of communication, its desired frequency and the level of detail that they expect. They can also assign responsibility for involving each stakeholder to a specific member of the team.

Table 5: Communications plan

What to communicate	Why	Preferred method	Responsibility	Frequency

Knowing the context will guide you in deciding who to approach, what methods to use, when to act and how best to frame your message. It can be helpful to consult with people who already understand this environment well.

Security professionals can define key interfaces and outcomes with target stakeholder groups. This is the foundation of the communication strategy.

Table 6: Example stakeholder interfaces

Interface	Interaction topics
Board	Development of overall security strategy Security enablement of business capabilities Security culture development
Executive Management	Translation of business needs into security roadmaps Reporting of overall security performance to business Financial planning (budgeting, forecasts and actuals reporting) Managing crisis scenarios and major security incidents
Management	Development of service integration processes and technology in line with the overall services portfolio Contracting with third parties (e.g. service providers)
Product team	Initiatives prioritisation Provision of security requirements Architecture and security guidance as part of ongoing changes and products Development of security enablers
Development team	Security guidelines and standards Incident response and issue resolution Implementation of security tooling Security advice and continual improvement

These interfaces can help tailor the message so security professionals speak the language of their target audience.

If the purpose of communication is to influence, then influencing tactics can be employed to increase effectiveness.

Influencing tactics can be grouped into two categories: core and supplementary.[34]

Core tactics:

1. Rational persuasion: Present clear evidence and logic to prove your initiative is feasible and vital for key business objectives.
2. Consultation: Invite input on improving or executing the plan – ownership drives buy-in.
3. Inspirational appeal: Link your request to individuals' core values, emotions or aspirations to spark genuine commitment.
4. Collaboration: Pledge support – offer tools, information or resources so we can succeed together.

Supplementary tactics

1. Apprising: Outline direct benefits – show how your initiative advances goals or eases workload.

[34] Yukl, G., Seifert, C. F. and Chavez, C., 2008, 'Validation of the Extended Influence Behavior Questionnaire', The Leadership Quarterly, vol. 19, no. 5, pp.609–621.

2. Ingratiation: Offer compliments or small acts of kindness to build goodwill before asking.
3. Exchange: Propose a clear quid pro quo – what do they want now or later in return for support.
4. Personal appeal: Leverage your relationship – ask for a favour.
5. Legitimising: Cite your authority or relevant policies to validate your request.
6. Pressure: Use reminders or firm prompts to nudge action – sparingly, to avoid backlash.
7. Coalition: Enlist and showcase allies' backing to demonstrate broad support.

Core tactics tend to work best across many situations. Supplementary tactics can strengthen your case when used carefully, but they also risk damaging relationships or trust if they're not chosen thoughtfully for the moment. By combining the right mix of core and supplementary tactics (guided by an environmental scan and ethical principles), security professionals will be better positioned to influence others effectively.

Cialdini's 'Six Principles of Persuasion'[35] is another framework that shows how tapping into common mental shortcuts can help influence people:

[35] Cialdini, R., 2001, 'Harnessing the Science of Persuasion', Harvard Business Review, vol. October 2001, pp.72–79.

1. Liking: Build rapport – genuinely praise, spotlight shared values and offer sincere compliments to boost agreement.
2. Reciprocity: Give first – share useful insights or small favours so others feel inclined to return the favour.
3. Social Proof: Highlight peers' actions – show that people like them have already embraced your idea.
4. Consistency: Remind them of past commitments or statements that align with your request to encourage follow-through.
5. Authority: Reference your expertise or respected endorsements to strengthen confidence in your initiative.
6. Scarcity: Stress limited availability to create urgency and prompt decision-making.

Attackers learned to use these principles to take advantage of people. They fake celebrity endorsements to scam people by exploiting Social Proof or leverage Authority by spoofing the CEO and demanding an urgent money transfer in business email compromise attacks. One study revealed that more than a third of participants voluntarily shared their password after being given a small incentive, leveraging Reciprocity.[36]

---

[36] Happ, C., Melzer, A. and Steffgen, G., 2016, 'Trick with treat–Reciprocity increases the willingness to communicate personal data', Computers in Human Behavior, 61, pp.372–377.

However, security professionals can use these tactics for good too. Leadership endorsements of security policies (Authority); normalising safe behaviour, e.g. "93% of employees updated their devices within 24 hours" (Social Proof); gaining public commitment for secure behaviours from staff (Consistency); building rapport through friendly communication (Liking); and helping solve people's problems (Reciprocity) are all examples of applying these principles to build a culture of security.

***

Being a security professional is first and foremost acting as a trusted advisor to the organisation. This includes understanding its objectives and aligning your efforts to support and enable delivery of the wider strategy.

It is also about articulating cyber risks and opportunities and working with the board and executive team on managing them.

This doesn't mean, however, that security professionals' role is to highlight security weaknesses and leave it to others to figure it all out. Instead, being someone people can turn to for advice is the best way to influence the direction and make the organisation more resilient against cyber threats.

For the advice to be effective, security professionals first need to earn the right to offer it. This takes trust.

The trust equation[37] is a simple yet powerful representation of what contributes to and hinders the trust-building process.

$$\text{Trust} = \frac{\textit{Credibility} + \textit{Reliability} + \textit{Intimacy}}{\textit{Self orientation}}$$

It's hard to trust someone's recommendations when they don't put our interests first and instead are preoccupied with being right or jump to solutions without fully understanding the problem.

Equally, as important as credibility is, a long list of the security professional's qualifications and experience on their own is not sufficient to be trustworthy. Having courage and integrity, following through on your promises and active listening, among other things, are key – "it is not enough to be right, you must also be helpful".[38]

Adapting the communication style to stakeholders' preferences helps build credibility and trust. Trust is what enables security professionals to add value, not by asking for more power, but by exercising influence.

The common mistake many security professionals make is jumping to influence or attempting behavioural change, for example with phishing simulations or security awareness campaigns, too soon, but this can be counterproductive.

---

[37] Maister, D.H., Galford, R. and Green, C., 2021, The Trusted Advisor, Free Press.
[38] Ibid.

The FBI Crisis Negotiation Unit's behavioural change model suggests that you first must invest in active listening, empathy and rapport:

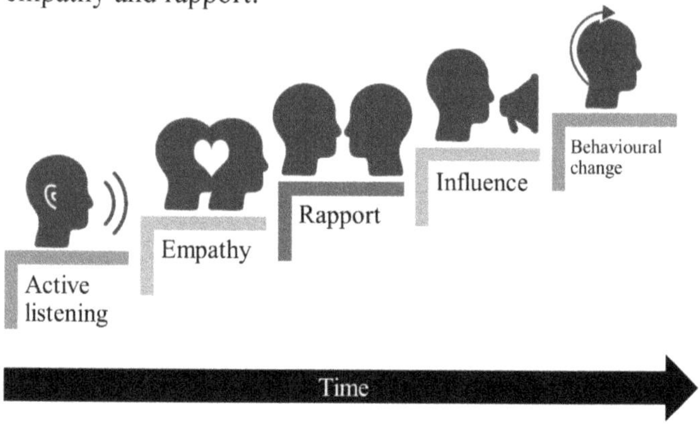

Figure 9: Behavioural change stairway model[39]

That's the reason we spent the first half of this book building on these important foundations: you can't skip any steps as consecutive efforts build on the previous ones.

The second half of the book will focus on designing better security mechanisms and changing behaviours to build the culture of security and protect the organisation from cyber threats.

d

[39] Vecchi, G.M., Van Hasselt, V.B. and Romano, S.J., 2005, 'Crisis (hostage) negotiation: Current strategies and issues in high-risk conflict resolution", Aggression and Violent Behavior, 10(5), pp.533–551.

CHAPTER 8: THE PSYCHOLOGY OF MANAGING CHANGE

Beyond communication and stakeholder management, security professionals need to be effective change agents to be successful. Cyber capability uplift and risk reduction initiatives often require significant organisational transformation and therefore call for deep capacity to deal with cognitive and emotional complexity.

Leadership of such complex initiatives requires orchestrating dialogue between the right people, at the right time, about the right issues. It calls for drawing on practical wisdom and judgement to progress complex challenges, navigating a pathway through power dynamics and negotiating project success based on a broad concept of value.[40]

In this chapter, we'll bring together the key principles we learned about so far in the form of an illustrative case study.

As a security professional, imagine that you identified an improvement opportunity to uplift cyber capability in your organisation. As this is likely to be a significant change, you follow Kotter's eight-step change management process[41] to increase the likelihood of success.

---

[40] Floris, M. and Cuganesan, S., 2019, 'Project leaders in transition: Manifestations of cognitive and emotional capacity', International Journal of Project Management, 37(3), pp.517–532.

[41] Kotter, J.P., 2007, 'Leading change: Why transformation efforts fail', Harvard Business Review, vol. 73, no. 2, pp.1–10.

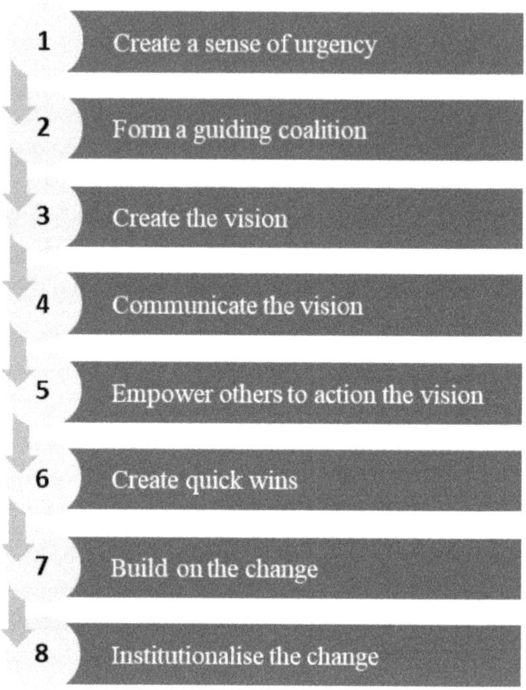

Figure 10: Kotter's eight steps

Step 1: Create a sense of urgency

Many organisations haven't experienced a major security incident in the past several years. However, the threat landscape is constantly evolving, with cyber attacks becoming more sophisticated. To keep pace, defences need to be strengthened and new security controls implemented.

The perceived absence of data breaches can create a sense of complacency among stakeholders. To get people out of their comfort zones, you perform a review of your security capabilities.

The assessment highlights critical deficiencies – the fact your organisation hasn't been breached can be largely attributed to luck.

You present the report to the executive leadership team: the case for urgent action is clear and maintaining the status quo is no longer a viable option. You reiterate your organisation's role in the wider ecosystem and the fact that attackers increased their capability and broadened their targeting.

You emphasise ethical leadership aspects and values.[42] You remind the leadership team that the effect on victims of data breaches can be shattering, including fraud and mental health impacts. You help the team see the organisation's wider responsibility: to protect your customers' data. This ethical lens helps reinforce the need for urgent action.

Step 2: Form a guiding coalition

You conduct your stakeholder analysis (use Figure 11 as an example). This reveals key stakeholder relationships and power structure in relation to this initiative, highlighting tension (lines with arrow heads) and indirect relationships (dotted lines).

---

[42] Hughes, M., 2016, 'Leading changes: Why transformation explanations fail', Leadership, vol. 12, no. 4, pp.449–469.

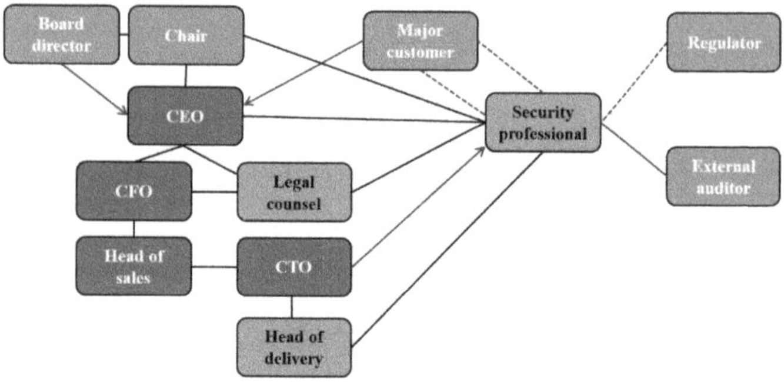

Figure 11: Example stakeholder analysis

This analysis informs the choice of key people to include in the guiding coalition.

You decide to form it with the CEO, the CFO, the CTO, the Head of delivery and Legal counsel. You request the CEO to sponsor the initiative and dedicate a leadership workshop to develop a shared understanding of the current state of your security capability. This also helps build commitment and further develop trust and communication between coalition members. All of you now share the sense of urgency and feel accountable for improving the security maturity.

Step 3: Create a vision

You co-create a vision statement for the initiative during the workshop with input from all guiding coalition members. It is fully aligned to the overall business mission and purpose.

You get input from the board, external auditor, regulator and a major customer, as key stakeholder, to achieve buy-in.

Security capability uplift is necessary to protect people's data and reduce the likelihood of data breaches. Despite being an ethical obligation to your customers, this change in itself has ethical, cultural and sustainability implications due to the technology that can be perceived by employees as potentially enabling unfair surveillance and high energy consumption; these risks can be assessed and mitigated as part of planning, as shown in Table 7.

Table 7: Top inherent risks and mitigation strategies

Risks	Severity	Probability	Actions to mitigate this risk
Ethical: Lack of transparency about new controls can create distrust among employees	High	Low	Develop policies and employee notice to ensure transparency. Consider additional communication
Ethical: Automated security controls may disproportionately affect people disadvantaged if not properly designed	High	Low	New automated security controls that avoid ethical concerns should be implemented as part of this project
Cultural: Controls that do not align with culture can create resistance or be seen as 'top-down'	Medium	High	Communicate the vision, emphasise the purpose and potential negative consequences of non-compliance
Cultural: Implementation of controls might disproportionately affect neurodivergent staff	Medium	Low	Engage HR business partner for accessibility and fairness considerations and input

Sustainability: Upgrading to new hardware for security purposes can result in increased e-waste	Medium	Low	Reuse existing hardware where possible. If not possible, work with supplier on recycling
Sustainability: Enhanced security energy consumption is higher than current baseline	Medium	Low	Most uplift initiatives relate to people and process with minimal impact on equipment-heavy consumption
Sustainability: Prioritising immediate security problems may deprioritise long-term sustainability goals	Medium	Low	Escalate potential prioritisation conflicts to CEO for decision

Step 4: Communicate the vision

You apply Authority and Social Proof persuasion principles[43] by getting the CEO to endorse the vision and demonstrate their support for the initiative. You also decided to add this vision statement to every presentation deck and update you provide. To maintain momentum and diversify communication channels, you arrange for the vision to be included in the monthly newsletter and added to onboarding materials for new joiners.

[43] Cialdini, R., 2001, 'Harnessing of the science of persuasion', Harvard Business Review, vol. October 2001, pp.72–79.

You pay particular attention to how you construct the message and how it's being received rather than solely focusing on quantity.[44] For example, you articulate the desired target state and what it means for people in your communications, bringing them on the journey.

You know you're on the right track when you observe the product managers role-modelling the vision and leading by example in the product backlog review meetings, where they prioritise security improvements to the product over other functionality that may be competing for limited resources.

You reflect on your communication style. People with a technical background tend to adopt a rational approach, focusing on facts. You decide to experiment more with inspirational appeal[45] to increase your impact through appealing to people's hearts as well as minds to increase the likelihood of change being successful.[46]

Step 5: Empower others to act on the vision

Security is often seen as an obstacle because it can create friction with core business processes. Your aim, however,

---

[44] Hughes, M., 2016, 'Leading changes: Why transformation explanations fail', Leadership, vol. 12, no. 4, pp.449–469.
[45] Yukl, G., Seifert, C.F. and Chavez, C, 2008, 'Validation of the extended influence behavior questionnaire', The Leadership Quarterly, vol. 19, no. 5, pp.609–621.
[46] Kotter, J.P., Akhtar, V. and Gupta, G, 2021, Change: How Organizations Achieve Hard-to-Imagine Results Despite Uncertain and Volatile Times, Wiley, Hoboken, New Jersey. Kotter, J.P, 2007, 'Leading change: Why transformation efforts fail', Harvard Business Review, vol. 73, no. 2, pp.1–10.

is to strengthen security while enabling business agility. You form partnerships with product and technology to understand common pain points where security gets in the way of productivity.

For example, you identify a policy that is overly restrictive without adding substantial security benefits, such as requesting people to change their passwords too often. You simplify this policy with no negative impact on security posture. This small yet significant change reduces the ongoing burden on employees and signals that people's concerns are heard.

You anticipate more barriers to be identified as your programme progresses and aim to remove these to empower people to experiment, encourage two-way communication, build buy-in and keep moving forward.

Step 6: Create quick wins

You proactively plan milestones and tangible improvements in security posture to maintain momentum. You develop a roadmap that helps the change appear less scary and more manageable.

It's common to struggle initially to articulate quick wins. You decide to outline smaller deliverables that serve as low hanging fruit for most initiatives. Such reframing allows you to create tangible milestones and communicate broadly about reaching them.

For example, you launch a new version of a risk dashboard and take your team out for lunch to celebrate. Several weeks into the project, you can demonstrate the progress visually, building on the initial current state assessment in Step 1.

You make quick wins feel more impactful by making them more relevant for the business. This increases the credibility of the initiative, brings more people onboard and shows to the wider group that change is possible.

Step 7: Build on the change

You use the momentum generated by quick wins to tackle harder, more complex security initiatives, like improving the detection and response capability. You are mindful, however, not to declare victory too soon – you keep emphasising the sense of urgency by reminding people of the threat landscape and risks. You regularly brief the executives and board on the current threat profile, key risks and the state of the improvement initiatives.

Although being more directive in your approach could yield short-term results, it often compromises long-term trust. For example, threatening disciplinary action in the event of non-compliance can be overused by security professionals.

Step 8: Institutionalise the change

Initially, you may not be able to fully embed this change in the organisational culture. The focus should be on demonstrating to stakeholders that new approaches and behaviours can lead to improved financial performance. For example:

- Protection of the bottom line though loss avoidance;

- Reduction in time spent managing security controls and associated overheads;
- Streamlined compliance effort;
- Reduction in cyber insurance premiums;
- Accelerated customer acquisition and retention due to increased trust;
- Expansion to new markets supported by a robust compliance regime and accreditation; and
- Launch of new resilient products.

You can also articulate material risk-reduction as a result of the implemented quick wins. This demonstrates that cyber capability uplift reduces the overall likelihood and impact of potential security incidents.

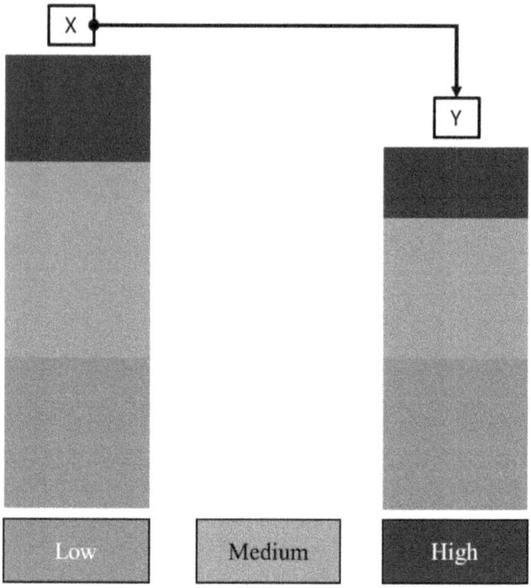

Figure 12: Example risk reduction

Going forward, you apply institutionalising change methods[47] to continue to ingrain new security attitudes within the organisation. Next, you focus on the following:

1. Control systems: Develop and enforce KPIs for executives to manage cyber risks, make acting in line with new values of protecting sensitive information a requirement for a promotion, embed security responsibilities in people's job descriptions, and incorporate questions about risk and security culture in the recruitment interview process.

[47] Johnson, G., Scholes, K. and Whittington, R., 2008, Exploring Strategy, 8th edn, Financial Times Prentice Hall.

2. Rituals and routines: Add a security sharing moment to the agenda of every organisation-wide meeting going forward, and offer an opportunity for interested staff to be upskilled on security and act as a security champion as a professional development benefit.
3. Stories: Organise lunch and learn sessions to tell stories of near misses and security events and what can be learned from them.

***

One of the key learnings is that a structured approach involving all of Kotter's eight steps is essential for successful transformation.

Time constraints may create a temptation to skip earlier steps – it's important to overcome this by remembering that avoiding steps only creates an impression of speed and can threaten long-term viability.[48] A clear vision, stakeholder engagement, constant communication and demonstrated progress increase the credibility of the initiative and lay a solid foundation for this change to be institutionalised.

[48] Kotter, J.P., 2007, 'Leading change: Why transformation efforts fail', Harvard Business Review, vol. 73, no. 2, pp.1–10.

CHAPTER 9: THE PSYCHOLOGY OF GOVERNANCE

Security regulation is evolving, increasing the breadth and depth of controls and rising fines. Customers, partners and regulators are increasing their focus on security and data protection.

The accelerated pace of change and technology adoption leads to high-impact systemic risks. New product strategy and innovation create new risks and compliance implications.

This means the security strategy itself needs to be flexible. It should respond by mitigating threats, meeting obligations and enabling organisational responsiveness.

Security professionals often operate in highly regulated environments and therefore must comply with numerous laws and regulations. They take this context into consideration while protecting the organisation's assets and mitigating risks. To do so, they establish desired practices that form the basis of company policies.

A policy is a document that provides a high-level overview of how business processes should operate in a secure manner. It defines the goal of the information security programme, which in turn supports the organisational vision, mission and strategy.

Such a high-level approach can be very beneficial in cases where a security professional wishes to describe the value of security, but it may also have limitations. The information can be too vague, or not well enough understood, to allow a particular control to be easily implemented. For example, stating that the network must be protected does not provide the necessary detail for a network security administrator to configure a firewall. It may create a scenario where security policies are not followed simply because they are not fully understood.

To support the policy, standards can be used to regulate the approach to security across an organisation, avoiding the implementation of conflicting or redundant solutions across various entities or departments.

A security professional might consider creating a set of guidelines to support the standards. Guidelines are not mandatory; they simply outline a set of good practices that people are encouraged to follow.

Security professionals will usually have to create a series of procedures: a set of steps that aid the implementation of policies and standards.

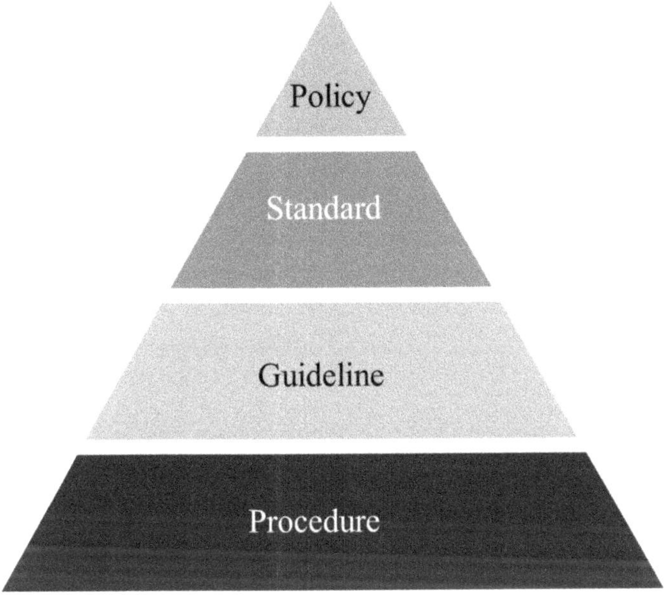

Figure 13: Policy hierarchy

For the purpose of this book, we will refer to all these documents as security policies.

***

A good starting point for developing a security policy is the ISO 27001 standard.[49] ISO 27001 provides guidance on managing the risk associated with threats to the confidentiality, integrity and availability of an organisation's assets.

These assets, as defined in ISO 27001, include people, software, hardware and services. According to the Standard, secure operation of the organisation can be achieved through creating and maintaining an information security management system (ISMS): a framework for risk management. It is usually supported by a set of information security policies.

Well-established frameworks such as ISO 27001 can be useful for implementing good practices and controls. However, using them purely as they appear on paper without adapting them to the organisation's specific characteristics can have negative consequences.

Security professionals might only stick to the Standard simply to achieve certification and demonstrate compliance. However, compliance doesn't equal security. An organisation may be unaware of risky practices its employees engage in, or may be implementing unnecessary controls suggested by the Standard that may hinder the overall performance. This contrasts with the business perspective, where the aim could be driving outcomes and not necessarily achieving perfect compliance.

---

[49] International Organization for Standardization, 2022, ISO/IEC 27001:2022 Information security, cybersecurity and privacy protection — Information security management systems — Requirements, Geneva.

Research suggests that there are challenges with security frameworks such as ISO 27001. For instance, such standards are too high-level and have an "abstract control definition", which "leaves space for interpretation". Furthermore, the study illustrates that many organisations focus solely on obtaining formal certification rather than implementing security controls that cater to their business needs.[50]

Another study concludes that ISO 27001 does not provide detailed guidance and requires substantial levels of expertise to implement: "If risk assessment is flawed, implementers don't have sufficient security and risk assessment expertise or do not have the management and organisational commitment to implement security, then it is perfectly possible to be fully compliant with the standard, but be insecure." [51]

Consequently, such implementations demonstrate poor return on investment. Or worse still, engage in security theatre.[52]

---

[50] Anttila, J. and Kajava, J. 2010, 'Challenging IS and ISM standardization for business benefits', Paper presented at ARES '10 International Conference on Availability, Reliability, and Security.

[51] Sharma, D. N. and Dash, P. K., 2012, 'Effectiveness of ISO 27001 as an information security management system: an analytical study of financial aspects', Far East Journal of Psychology and Business, 9(5), pp. 57–71.

[52] Schneier (2003, p. 38) defines *security theater* as "the practice of investing in countermeasures intended to provide the feeling of improved security while doing little or nothing to actually achieve it."

An example of that is a risk register that is only looked at once a year, just before an audit: this is tick-the-box compliance. A risk register should be a living document that supports ongoing risk and control effectiveness monitoring. It's a communication tool with multiple stakeholders, particularly the ones with risk accountability.

When creating a security policy, security professionals might choose a standard framework to work from, but they should do so only as a starting point. The challenge is that people in their organisations may not even be aware that such a document exists or where to find it.

This shouldn't come as a surprise, since corporate policies are consistently mentioned as being the greatest cause of dissatisfaction in the workplace. A poorly designed corporate policy, as one of 'hygiene' factors, tends to demotivate people.[53]

This finding was proven at Texas Instruments Incorporated, where a random selection of scientists, engineers, manufacturing supervisors, technicians and assemblers were chosen from within the Dallas divisions.[54] Each staff member was asked to think of a time when they felt exceptionally good or exceptionally bad about their job, either in the past or the present. The participants would describe a favourable and unfavourable circumstance and whether the effect on their emotions was long-lasting.

---

[53] Herzberg, F., Mausner, B. and Snyderman, B. B., 1993, The motivation to work, new edn, Transaction.

[54] Scott, M. M., 1964, 'Who are your motivated workers?', Harvard Business Review, pp. 73–88.

The results demonstrate that *achievement* was the most popular category, accounting for a third of all responses. Company *policy* and administration, which can be thought of as the perception of an organisation's procedures and practices, was expressed unfavourably four times more frequently than favourably.

***

Imagine an experiment where five monkeys were put in a room with bananas hanging from the ceiling. A pole was placed in the middle to access the bananas.[55]

Each time a monkey tried to climb the pole, the rest of the monkeys were soaked with cold water. After a few repetitions, the monkeys started to physically reprimand whoever climbed the pole. Naturally, no monkey dared to go up the pole again.

Scientists then took one of the monkeys out of the room and replaced it with another one. The new monkey saw the bananas and tried to reach them by climbing the pole, but was disciplined immediately by the others. Although confused, the new member learned not to climb the pole.

A second monkey was then substituted with a new one and the story repeated. Eventually, all the monkeys were replaced by new ones. Although none of these monkeys had themselves received a cold shower, they continued to

---

[55] Hamel, G. and Prahalad, C. K., 1996, Competing for the future, Harvard Business Press.

deter anyone who attempted to reach the bananas, accepting the fact that things are done in a particular way.

This experiment never took place in real life, but it illustrates an important point: security professionals may develop similar behaviour if they don't challenge the status quo and don't ask why policies are implemented in a certain way.

When policies are put in place without clear guidance or further scrutiny, an organisation can develop problems. Although it may seem to comply with all relevant regulations, beneath the surface people may be struggling to get their job done and may be forced to violate those poorly implemented security policies.

Let's consider a situation where a security professional is required to develop a policy that protects their organisation from malware.

According to control 8.7 of ISO 27001:2022, "Protection against malware shall be implemented and supported by appropriate user awareness."[56]

The following section provides guidance recommended by the ISO 27002 standard.[57] It also presents scenarios that

[56] International Organization for Standardization, 2022, ISO/IEC 27001:2022 Information security, cybersecurity and privacy protection — Information security management systems — Requirements, Geneva.

[57] International Organization for Standardization, 2022, ISO/IEC 27002:2022 Information security, cybersecurity and privacy protection — Information security controls, Geneva.

demonstrate how these controls may impact employees' behaviour.

***

1. Implementing rules that prevent or detect the use of unauthorised software.

In practice it might mean that if people wish to install software that is not on the authorised list, they must gain formal written approval from the security team.

Here's how this policy affected Alex, a financial analyst:

> Alex is writing a report for a client. The deadline is fast approaching but they still have a lot of work. The night before the deadline, Alex realises that to finish their work, they require special data analysis software that is not included in the list of authorised programs.
>
> They are unable to install it on their workstation because they don't have the required permissions. Getting formal written approval from the security department is not feasible, because it will take too long.
>
> Alex decides to copy the sensitive information required for the analysis onto their personal laptop to finish the work at home, where they can install and use any software they want. They understand the risk, but they also want to get the job done to avoid missing the deadline and get a good performance review.

Their personal laptop, however, doesn't have the same security requirements as the work one. When they accidentally download and run a malicious attachment, sensitive data ends up getting stolen.

2. Establishing protective measures against risks associated with obtaining files and software either from or via external networks or on any other medium.

Here is a potential implementation of this policy: if people want to obtain a specific file from the Internet or from an external device, they must submit a written request to their manager, who will decide if this file is essential to performing their duties.

Here's how this policy affected Diego:

Diego is a consultant working closely with an international energy company to finalise a report on a risk analysis that he performed.

He works directly with the CFO of this company, who is very impatient and busy with other priorities.

Diego doesn't want to annoy her, because she may complain to his line manager. This is a very important client, which brings a large amount of revenue to Diego's organisation.

The client is not aware of a new policy, which was recently implemented by the security department, and uploads important pieces of information to a file sharing portal in an encrypted archive because it is too big to transfer over corporate email. This file sharing portal is not approved in Diego's organisation.

She communicates the password to Diego over the phone and sends him the link.

Diego feels that he cannot explain the new policy to the client, but is unable to access the files required to finalise his report.

He decides to go to the library during his lunch break and downloads the important file to a USB from there. He understands the risk, but believes that getting all the necessary approvals may take too long.

At the library, Diego not only downloads the encrypted files but also opens them on the public machine to check their integrity as he does not want to have to return later in the day if there's an issue with the password.

Because the library is far from the office and he hasn't had his lunch yet, he hurries and forgets to delete the decrypted file from the machine in the library.

Diego realises his mistake when he's back in the office, but reasons that it is not a big deal and nothing bad can happen.

3. Conducting regular automated validation of the software and data content of systems, investigating any unapproved files or unauthorised amendments.

If unauthorised data or software is found during such checks, the employee in question is given a warning. Repeated warnings for non-compliance with this policy can be considered potential grounds for dismissal.

Here's how this policy affected Priya:

Priya uses data and files obtained from various sources in her analysis. She is not sure if it is all approved. She's afraid to clarify this situation with the security team due to the potential disciplinary action.

To avoid being caught using these files, Priya stores the information on her personal laptop.

After some time, however, she realises that it takes too long to copy and delete data from her corporate machine to her personal laptop and vice versa, and decides to process all the information, including the sensitive information, on her personal laptop instead.

Unfortunately, Priya leaves her bag with her personal laptop in a taxi. She never tells anyone about this incident to avoid embarrassment.

4. Installing and regularly updating malware detection and repair software to scan computers and electronic storage media.

Here's how this policy affects Mei:

Mei is a derivatives trader who carries out thousands of deals every day. Time and efficiency are critical success factors for her.

The new malware detection software slows her workstation's performance. This directly affects her job, as she is unable to act as fast as before and misses many valuable opportunities.

Mei understands the risk of malware but is also frustrated by her inability to work efficiently.

She finds a way to manually disable the malware detection software on her computer.

While doing research on the Internet, Mei accidentally clicks a malicious link and unwittingly introduces malware into the network, with no software installed to stop the infection.

5. Providing awareness or training to all users on how to identify and potentially mitigate the receipt, sending or installation of malware-infected emails, files or programs.

The security department rolls out online learning to meet compliance requirements. The program is the same for everyone, regardless of roles and responsibilities.

The training is not engaging and not tailored to the organisation's context and needs.

Employees are not paying attention, clicking through the content as they cannot see the benefit to their primary roles or overall protection of the organisation.

As a result, employees lack knowledge, skills and motivation to report potentially malicious emails, increasing the risk of a successful phishing attack.

The above examples illustrate the potential negative outcomes of implementing controls short-sightedly with the sole purpose of complying with the ISO 27001 standard. The policy had an inadvertent impact on people trying to do their job. This resulted in them putting their organisations at risk.

When security professionals fail to scrutinise blanket controls before putting them into practice, employees may come under additional strain due to their increased workload, preventing them from performing their core business tasks, and therefore they may find ways to circumvent security measures. The best hackers are employees simply trying to do their job.

CHAPTER 10: THE SECURITY PROFESSIONALS' PERSPECTIVE

Previous case studies demonstrate that security professionals often fail to consider how the policies they put in place could affect the day-to-day activities of employees.

Lack of clear guidance when designing and implementing security mechanisms, and the fact that they must resort to their own judgement, makes the problem even more difficult to solve.

First, we need to understand whether security professionals perceive this as a problem. To explore this further, a number of interviews were conducted with security leaders of major global organisations.[58]

All these experts had seven or more years of work experience in the field of information security and were holding managerial positions at the time of the interview. Answers were anonymised to preserve the privacy of the participants.

The main goal was to gather insight into information security leaders' awareness of the fact that decisions regarding the particular implementation of security controls affect organisations as a whole, and that their actions may negatively impact employee performance.

---

[58] Zinatullin, L., 2013, 'Modelling conflicts between security compliance and human behaviour', dissertation, University College London.

The findings confirm that security leaders mostly use their own judgement and experience regarding the implementation of particular information security controls.

"When I'm making a decision to implement some aspect of the ISO 27001 standard in my organisation," one security manager stated, "much of the decision centres on what the particular implementation would actually look like. ISO 27001 is very high-level and is by all means not a policy in itself – it just gives you one or two criteria or one or two suggestions as to how your security policies should look. As a result of the freedom of implementation, you actually have to write the policies yourself."

Security managers also understand the role of involving business management in the process of implementing security controls.

"If there is no benefit to the business, you don't do it," another expert mentioned. "You should start with the business – find the people who these controls directly affect and get their buy-in."

A common theme was that business objectives should always be the priority. "Many security managers think that security is the most important thing. I personally don't think so," one manager admitted. "Paying shareholders is more important. Inhibiting those activities or encouraging dangerous activities because of what you are doing makes the situation worse."

There is also awareness among security leaders of how to detect non-compliance. "I walk around the building on occasion," one expert revealed. "I wiggle doors and I check workstations for locked screens. The other way to gain insight into compliance is through rumours or chatting with people."

Most interviewed security leaders agree that one should not punish people for non-compliance. One must first understand the root cause of the problem. For instance, one expert suggested, "You don't react to non-compliance with anger, you try to find out why it happened, rather than just the fact that it has failed. Moreover, you use it as a possible trigger for education and awareness and possibility for improvement."

Another expert reinforced this view: "At the end of the day it failed because, with high probability, you implemented it badly, because you forced some particular way of working or method which your employees can't use, so they worked around it."

Another common theme was that information security managers are, to a certain degree, aware of the impact of the security policy on people's behaviour. "Yes, I think I'm aware of the impact of my policies," one security manager said, "because when it affects users in a negative way, we hear about it. There are lots of complaints."

A number of information security leaders backed up their statements with examples: "Some people want to look at a spreadsheet or use an application on their personal tablets but can't, because security controls don't allow access to the business applications via a tablet. So they have to use a laptop rather than a device of their own choice, and they are unhappy. So yes, we are aware of such tension."

These interviews suggest that this awareness is directly related to the number of complaints.

Several security leaders stated that it is difficult to assess the impact of security controls on people's behaviour: "We never measured it," one manager admitted. "We don't have a way of measuring it. So we don't know."

This view was echoed: "It is one thing to put controls in place and another to measure effectiveness. When it comes to users it is very difficult. They are not like servers, where you can look at, for example, CPU performance before and after some change."

A subsequent theme emerged: whether security managers are aware of employees' daily business activities. It appears that they are, but only to the degree required to successfully manage their security initiatives.

One security leader said, "At a high level we are aware; at the detailed process level really only when we are doing a project in that department, when we need to understand the processes within our project."

Another example that supports the same argument was brought up: "There are situations where we do a particular project on a new system. For example, if we are working on a new credit card system which is being implemented, we work through the people's roles and we work through the general data storage, so we become familiar with the supporting department's employee activities."

The results illustrate that several participants believe they can understand people's day-to-day business activities and implement security controls accordingly.

All the interviewed leaders agreed that the knowledge of what staff are doing can help them improve the implementation of information security policies. The majority of security leaders understand the importance of involving people and assessing the possible impact on their behaviour when deciding how to implement particular security controls. However, they also agree that their awareness of business activities of staff is reactive and based mainly on complaints.

We've heard from security leaders, but the analysis is not complete until we have compared these views to those of the employees themselves.

CHAPTER 11: THE EMPLOYEE PERSPECTIVE

It is not easy to gain insight into employee behaviour without contributions from people who are willing and able to honestly share their opinion on information security issues.

Researchers conducted a series of interviews and identified three common reasons for non-compliance, shown in Figure 14[59].

They built strong relationships with a number of organisations in the telecommunications and energy sectors, which readily allowed access to their employees for the purposes of studying their compliance behaviour. The employees were assured that no sanctions would be imposed as a result of their participation.

---

59 Kirlappos, I., Beautement, A. and Sasse, M. A., 2013, ''Comply or die' is dead: long live security-aware principal agents', in Financial Cryptography and Data Security, Springer, pp. 70–82.

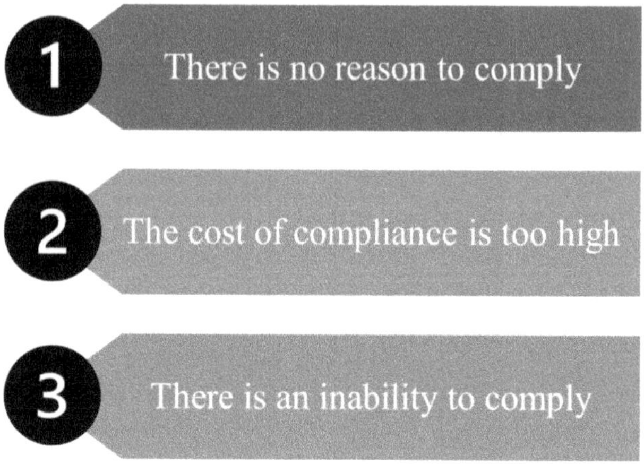

Figure 14: Common reasons for non-compliance

Let's examine each reason in more detail.

1. There is no clear reason to comply

The research results revealed that employees usually don't have an accurate concept of what information security is and what it aims to protect. They tend to lack a clear understanding of what certain security policies forbid and allow, which often leads to the creation of security myths. Even in those rare cases where employees are aware of a security policy and interpret it correctly, the motivation to comply is still lacking.

Non-security professionals are unlikely to be aware of the impact of their behaviour or to understand the associated risks. However, because following a policy involves effort, and if there is no immediate threat, non-compliant behaviour can appear to be the more attractive and comfortable option.

The study reveals typical examples of unintentional non-compliant behaviour. For example, employees seldom consider that deleted data can be recovered from drives that have been lost or stolen. They lack awareness that deleting data after completing a file transfer does not always provide adequate protection. Furthermore, it is widely believed that the data stored on company laptops is secure because a password is required to gain access, but they are unaware that, in some instances, the data may be unencrypted and can be retrieved from the hard drive. This leads to the risky practice of storing sensitive data locally on laptops when travelling on public transport. What is also largely overlooked is that employees rarely consider that their actions might enable malware to enter their organisation's systems through their personal USB sticks.

2. The cost of compliance is too high

The majority of employees are hired to perform specific jobs, such as marketing, managing projects, manufacturing goods or overseeing financial investment. Their main, sometimes only, priority will be the efficient completion of their core business activity, so information security will usually only be a secondary consideration. Consequently, employees will be reluctant to invest more than limited effort and time on a secondary task that they rarely understand and from which they perceive no benefit.

When security mechanisms cause additional workload, employees will favour non-compliant behaviour to complete their primary tasks quickly.

There is a lack of awareness among security leaders about the burden that security mechanisms impose on employees, because it is assumed that people can easily accommodate the effort that security compliance requires.[60] Once security controls cross a certain point of complexity, people push back and find workarounds. In many organisations, they've long since reached that breaking point.[61]

Employees tend to experience a negative impact on their performance because they feel that these, often cumbersome, security mechanisms drain both their time and effort. From their perspective, the risk mitigation achieved through compliance is not worth the disruption to their productivity. In extreme cases, the more urgent the delivery of the primary task, the more appealing and justifiable non-compliance becomes, regardless of employees being aware of the risks. For example, computers in hospital emergency rooms are often left unlocked by staff – violating security policies – who prioritise the immediate treatment of patients to save their lives over the protection of their data.[62]

When security mechanisms hinder or significantly slow employees' performance, they will cut corners, and reorganise and adjust their primary tasks, to avoid them. This seems to be particularly prevalent in file sharing, especially when people are restricted by permissions or

---

[60] Beautement, A., Sasse, M.A. and Wonham, M., 2008, September, 'The compliance budget: managing security behaviour in organisations', in proceedings of the 2008 New Security Paradigms workshop, pp. 47–58.

[61] Herley, C., 2013, 'More is not the answer', IEEE Security & Privacy, 12(1), pp.14–19.

[62] ENISA, 'Smart Hospitals: Security and Resilience for Smart Health Service and Infrastructures', 2016.

time-consuming protocols. People will usually work around the security mechanisms and resort to the readily available commercial alternatives, which may be unsafe.

From the employee's perspective, the consequences of not completing a primary task are severe, as opposed to the consequences of the risk associated with breaching security policies.

3. There is an inability to comply

There can be cases in which enforced compliance fails to be an option for employees, even when they are more than willing to invest their time and effort. In such cases, the predominant scenario is that people cannot comply because the security mechanisms do not match their basic requirements.

It is common to see people copying files onto laptops because remote accessibility is problematic, or because their network drive capacity is insufficient.

Another recurring issue is a requirement for numerous passwords to access different corporate systems, all of which employees tend to have difficulty in memorising. People will 'fix' this problem by reusing their passwords or storing them insecurely.

People tend to be aware of how their behaviour can pose an increased risk but feel justified in finding these workarounds because the organisation has failed to provide them with an appropriate technical implementation. They assume that the organisation would rather allow security violations than stop the main business process – an opinion often adopted by managerial staff. When everybody shares this inadequate and risky perspective, the organisation is an accomplice in the employees' unsafe behaviour.

The implementation of security compliance creates a strain and enlarges the gap between security teams and the rest of the organisation. Employees tend to develop a negative view of information security in general and respond to security enforcers with scepticism or may simply ignore them. This bias can easily discourage employees from behaving in a secure manner, regardless of how sensibly designed security controls may be.

***

Preventing phishing is a case in point. Relying solely on training is both inefficient and ineffective.[63] Clicking links is fundamental to modern work, so expecting people to scrutinise every message overloads their day. People click for many reasons, from individual traits to situational pressures like tight deadlines or high stress.[64]

---

[63] Ho, G., Mirian, A., Luo, E., Tong, K., Lee, E., Liu, L., Longhurst, C. A., Dameff, C., Savage, S. and Voelker, G. M., 2025, 'Understanding the efficacy of phishing training in practice', in 2025 IEEE Symposium on Security and Privacy (SP), pp. 37–54, IEEE.

[64] Williams, E.J., Beardmore, A. and Joinson, A.N., 2017, 'Individual differences in susceptibility to online influence: A theoretical review', Computers in Human Behavior, 72, pp.412–421.

Simulated phishing tests may yield neat metrics, but they have serious drawbacks too. No one can reliably spot every fake email, and punishing mistakes borders on entrapment – demoralising staff and damaging trust. When employees fear blame, they hide errors instead of reporting them, robbing security professionals of critical early warnings.

When people slip up, the goal is not punishment but rapid remediation. By building a security culture grounded in support, security professionals can encourage employees to admit mistakes – picking up the phone to the security team rather than hoping the incident goes unnoticed. That open dialogue speeds response and positions security professionals as enablers, not enforcers.

Security professionals must broaden the anti-phishing strategy by pairing strong technical safeguards with targeted education.

A layered defence approach should block as many malicious messages as possible before they reach people, then empower employees to recognise and report anything that slips past those barriers.

Mechanisms should be put in place to neutralise the impact of any undetected phishing emails and build rapid-response capabilities so that when an incident does occur, security professionals can help investigate, contain and recover with minimal disruption.

***

Overly complicated security mechanisms are usually implemented at the cost of the organisation's productivity, because they tend to consume valuable employee resources. It is not unusual to find that important parts of the organisation will foster insecure practices, because they value productivity over security and don't perceive any immediate risk.

Employees generally try to comply with an organisation's security policies, but, most importantly, they simply want to get their work done. Sometimes employees may violate an organisation's security policy through malicious behaviour, but it is often because of poor control implementation that does not consider their needs.

Here is where the job of an information security professional gets interesting. When an action that increases the organisation's cyber risk is identified, they should first rule out the possibility of malicious behaviour, and then should understand where and why the security policy failed to work properly, forcing the employees to find workarounds.

The more a security policy implementation facilitates employee values and priorities, the better it fosters employee incentives and strengthens the security culture.

To achieve alignment between security and employee perspective, the process of formulating security policies must be focused on employee behaviour. Security professionals must remember that employee performance is goal-oriented.

These goals are usually focused on business processes and their demands, and are generally seen as completely independent of information security goals, which are often perceived as abstract and lacking context.

When the viewpoint of employees is not taken into account, the result is their partial or total absence in the process of designing security mechanisms. This often leads to, or enhances, the vicious cycle of developing an inadequate security culture, which in turn reinforces the misguided perception of security and the unsafe behaviour that comes with it. In this scenario, security mechanisms can be considered to have a direct negative impact on employees' routine jobs. To avoid this, employee behaviour must be considered.

CHAPTER 12: THE PSYCHOLOGY OF HUMAN BEHAVIOUR

The human decision-making process is the preferred subject of psychologists and economists. Historically, they viewed human behaviour as regular and highly predictable. This helped the researchers build various models to comprehend social and economic phenomena. Such systems were compared to reliable pendulum clocks: one can take them apart and observe how the pieces fit together.[65]

People, however, are much more complicated. Their behaviour, which is considered "highly irregular and disorderly", has more in common with clouds, which are harder to predict due to their dynamic and constantly changing nature. Various theories were developed to understand the drivers underlying certain actions. Such findings have been adopted by information security researchers to understand human behaviour in relation to risk mitigation.

One of the dominant theories relating to human behaviour is *rational choice*. This provides insight into social and economic behaviour, and reveals how people aim to maximise their personal benefits and minimise their costs. Personal gain tends to be the main motivator: people make

---

[65] Popper, K. R., 1972, Of clocks and clouds: an approach to the problem of rationality and the freedom of man, in Objective knowledge: an evolutionary approach, Clarendon Press, pp. 206–265.

decisions based on the perceived benefit as well as the cost of the outcome, and act accordingly.

This theory can also be used to explain how employees make decisions about unsafe security practices: it may be rational for people not to comply with a security policy, because the effort outweighs the perceived level of risk reduction.

One study, for example, observed frequent insecure computer-related practices among university students, which included revealing passwords, downloading potentially unsafe attachments and not backing up their data.[66]

Although the students were familiar with safe computing behaviour, they continued to exhibit risky conduct.

The researchers conclude that organisations may have to go a step further than simply recommending safe practices: compliance may have to be imposed more forcefully.

To explore whether the punishment can indeed be effective, let's look at the *theory of general deterrence.*

This theory suggests that people will not comply with the rules if they know that breaking them will not be followed by punishment. Before elaborating, it is worth defining the terms *intrinsic* and *extrinsic motivation.*

Intrinsic motivation comes from within the individual, which usually leads to engaging in behaviour that is

[66] Aytes, K. and Connolly, T., 2004, 'Computer and risky computing practices: A rational choice perspective', Journal of Organizational End User Computing, 16(2), pp. 22–40.

personally rewarding. In this context, people are not driven by the idea of an external incentive, but by their own desires.

Extrinsic motivation, on the other hand, results from the hope of gaining an external reward or avoiding punishment for their conduct.

Table 8: Extrinsic vs. intrinsic motivation factors

Extrinsic	Intrinsic
Rewards	Meaning
Fear of punishment	Enjoyment
Competition	Interest

A study refers to an extended version of the theory of general deterrence to find out if information security awareness training affects the perception of company sanctions in terms of severity and certainty.[67] The researchers studied employees from eight different companies who had received such training and were aware of monitoring software on their machines. Their findings show that the perception of punishment is more effective in deterring risky behaviour than imposing sanctions.

[67] D'Arcy, J., Hovav, A. and Galletta, D., 2009, 'User awareness of security countermeasures and its impact on information systems misuse: A deterrence approach', Information Systems Research, 17(1), pp. 79–98.

However, other researchers challenged the significance of these findings, which use the theory of general deterrence to deal with and predict behaviour related to compliance, because the approaches that are suggested are solely based on extrinsic motivation.[68] They state that this model doesn't consider intrinsic motivation, which is an important aspect and strong driving force of the human character.

Instead, they propose a model that includes both the intrinsic and extrinsic motivators of human behaviour. Their analysis revealed that approaches relating to the intrinsic motivation paradigm led to a significant increase in compliant behaviour over approaches relating to the extrinsic motivation model.

Another theory, *cognitive evaluation*, supports the importance of intrinsic motivation. It can be used to predict the effects that rewards have on intrinsic motivation, specifically when these rewards are of a tangible nature, such as awards and prizes, as opposed to verbal rewards or recognition.

Following this theory, when rewards are perceived as a means of controlling behaviour, they have a negative effect on intrinsic motivation. A recipient's sense of autonomy and self-determination will decline when they feel that they are being controlled.

The cognitive evaluation theory also explains why verbal or non-tangible rewards have positive effects on intrinsic motivation. For employees to feel increasingly like they are

---

[68] Son, J.-Y., 2011, 'Out of fear or desire? Toward a better understanding of employees' motivation to follow IS security policies', Information Management, 48(7), pp. 296–302.

skilful at completing certain tasks and that their performance has been positively evaluated by their supervisors, non-tangible rewards of this type must be delivered in a way that is not perceived as coercive. This type of reward system would boost employees' performance and determination because of increased intrinsic motivation.

Within the information security context, this theory recommends adopting a positive, non-tangible reward system to build secure habits.

All the above theories suggest that to effectively protect organisations' assets, security professionals should consider people's motivations and attitudes.

Security controls should be designed in a way that reduces the mental and physical workload of staff by fostering intrinsic motivation, while reducing extrinsic motivation or deterrence.

Security professionals must keep employees' perspectives in mind and at the very core of their approaches to designing security mechanisms.

CHAPTER 13: SECURITY AND USABILITY

One of the main contributing factors to insecure practices by people is an extensive workload caused by poorly developed and implemented security controls. Security mechanisms that are designed with people's perspective in mind is the solution.

People's resources are limited, and they tend to struggle with making effective decisions when they are overwhelmed.

This was demonstrated in an experiment[69] where the participants were divided into two groups: the first group was asked to memorise a two-digit number (e.g. 54) and the second group was asked to remember a longer seven-digit number (e.g. 4509672). The researchers then asked them to go down the hall to the other room to collect their reward for participating. This payment, however, could only be received if the number was recalled correctly.

Along the corridor, they encountered another experimenter, who offered them either fruit or a less healthy chocolate option. They were told that they could collect their chosen option after they finish the experiment, but they had to decide there and then.

The results demonstrated that people who were given the easier task of remembering a two-digit number mostly chose the healthy option, while people overburdened by the

---

[69] Shiv, B. and Fedorikhin, A., 1999, 'Heart and mind in conflict: the interplay of affect and cognition in consumer decision making', Journal of Consumer Research, pp. 278–292.

more challenging task of recalling a longer string of digits succumbed to the more gratifying chocolate.

The implications of these findings, however, are not only limited to dieting. Another study[70] looked at the decision-making patterns of judges when considering inmates for parole during different stages of the day.

Despite rejecting parole being the default decision, in the mornings and after lunch judges had more cognitive capacity and energy to fully consider the details of the case and make an informed decision, resulting in more frequently granted paroles. In the evenings, judges tended to reject parole far more frequently, which is believed to be due to mental strain. They simply ran out of energy and defaulted to the safest option.

How can this be applied in the information security context? Security professionals should bear in mind that if people are stressed at work, making difficult decisions, engaging in their primary business activities, they get tired.

This might affect their ability or willingness to maintain secure behaviours. In a corporate context, this cognitive depletion may result in staff defaulting to core business tasks at the expense of secondary security responsibilities, making the scenarios described in Chapter 9 a real possibility.

When people perform tasks that are aligned with their own mental models – the natural way that they view the world

---

[70] Danziger, S., Levav, J. and Avnaim-Pesso, L., 2011, 'Extraneous factors in judicial decisions', Proceedings of the National Academy of Sciences, 108(17), pp. 6889–6892.

and how they expect it to work – the activities present less of a cognitive challenge than those that work against these models.

If people can apply their knowledge and experience to a problem, less energy is required to solve it in a secure manner and they are less mentally depleted.

Security professionals should pay attention to the usability of security mechanisms, aligning them with people's existing mental models.

Relating to an existing experience is highlighted in an example of the desktop metaphor introduced by Xerox researchers in the 1980s.[71] People were able to relate to the graphical computer interface as opposed to the command line. They could manipulate objects similarly to the way they do with the physical desk: store and categorise files in folders as well as move, rename or delete by placing them in the recycle bin.

Building on existing mental models makes the adoption of new technologies and ways of working easier. However, such mappings must consider cultural background. The metaphor might not work if it is not part of the existing mental model. For instance, Apple Macintosh's original trash icon was difficult to recognise in Japan, where people were not accustomed to metallic bins of that kind.

In security, many people may not have an accurate mental model of how encryption works: they see a lock icon and

[71] Maeda, J., 2006, The Laws of Simplicity, MIT Press.

assume it means the site is safe, not just that the connection is encrypted.

Relating to the right model, therefore, can enhance security. For example, when suggesting multifactor authentication (MFA), the interface may use analogies, e.g. "think of your phone as a key".

Good interface design not only lightens the burden on people but can also complement security. Traditionally, it was assumed that security and usability always contradict each other: security makes things more complicated, while usability aims to improve the user experience. In reality, they can support each other by defining safe and unsafe activities. Effective design should make safe activities simple to perform while hindering unsafe ones.

For example, drop-down menus or checkbox lists for permissions constrain choices to valid options, preventing arbitrary or malformed input.

Good security design applies constraints where they're needed, but pairs those limits with clear, timely feedback and usable alternatives, so people can follow the process rather than work around or abandon it.

Imagine entering an MFA code and seeing no confirmation – it's natural to try multiple codes in quick succession or even disable MFA out of frustration.

Immediate feedback is vital: the system must clearly report on what happened after each action. When changing a password or enabling MFA, the interface should confirm with messages like "Your password has been changed" or "MFA is now active".

Such feedback closes the loop on performed actions and builds the correct mental model of the security mechanism.

Effective security design leverages affordances[72] so people don't have to guess how to use something. For instance, a visible "Enable MFA" toggle that looks interactive (with a clear "on/off" state) encourages people to activate it.

Conversely, hidden or non-intuitive controls drive people away from security. Research shows that most people could not correctly encrypt an email, despite an attractive interface, confirming that standard design techniques alone are insufficient for security.[73]

Even the most technically skilled stakeholders – software developers – often lack the support and resources needed to build secure systems. Studies demonstrate that security modules, such as cryptographic libraries, are hard to use correctly[74], and the pressure to deliver features means developers rarely have time to deeply research or thoroughly test their code as security professionals recommend.

Rather than expecting developers to trade speed for security, a more effective strategy is to supply them with

---

72 Norman, D.A., 1988, The Psychology of Everyday Things, Basic Books.

73 Whitten, A. and Tygar, J.D., 1999, August, 'Why Johnny Can't Encrypt: A Usability Evaluation of PGP 5.0', in USENIX security symposium, vol. 348, pp.169–184.

74 Fahl, A., Harbach, M., Perl, H., Kötter, M. and Smith, M., 2013, 'Rethinking SSL development in an appified world', Proceedings of the 2013 ACM Conference on Computer and Communications Security (CCS'13).

well-designed, secure components and clear usage examples that integrate seamlessly into their workflows.[75]

Security needs to fit into work processes rather than disrupt them. This requires the involvement of security professionals early in the design process. Security and usability shouldn't be extra features introduced as an afterthought once the system has been developed, but an integral part of the design from the beginning.

Security professionals can provide input into the design process via iterative or participatory design[76], where key stakeholders are involved in defining requirements, testing and evaluation.

Security doesn't fail because people don't care – it fails because systems don't care about people. When security controls align with how people think, work and decide – especially under pressure – they become invisible allies rather than obstacles. The path to secure behaviour isn't paved with stricter rules, but with empathy and design that works with people, not against them. Build security for people, and people will build security with you.

---

[75] Acar, Y., Backes, M., Fahl, S., Kim, D., Mazurek, M. and Stransky, S., 2016, 'You get where you're looking for: The impact of information sources on code security', Proceedings of the 2016 IEEE Symposium on Security and Privacy (Oakland'16).

[76] For iterative design, see Nielsen, J., 1993, 'Iterative user interface design', IEEE Computer, 26(11), pp. 32–41.

CHAPTER 14: SOLVING COMPLEX SECURITY PROBLEMS

Including security requirements from the very start is not enough to solve a particular security-usability issue. This is because such problems can be described as *wicked.*

A wicked problem in the context of social policy planning is defined as a challenging, if not impossible, one to solve due to missing, poorly defined or inconsistent requirements from stakeholders, which may morph over time with no optimal solution.[77]

[77] Rittel H.W.J and Webber M.M., 'Dilemmas in a General Theory of Planning', Policy Sciences, 4, 1973, pp.155–169.

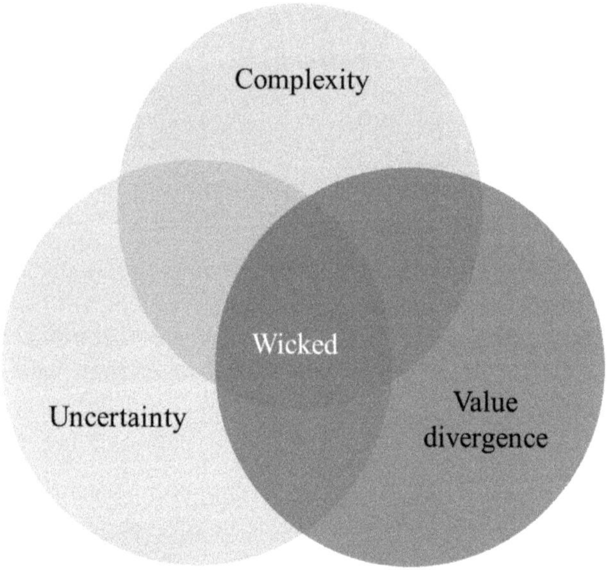

Figure 15: Wicked problem[78]

These are stubborn challenges that refuse to bow to straightforward analysis or top-down commands. At their core, they weave together complexity, uncertainty, constant change and deep conflict in ways that defy the neat solutions found in textbooks.

Unlike simply complicated tasks, where many pieces may need assembling but the relationships between them are known, wicked problems bind their components so tightly

[78] Head, B.W., 2022, Wicked Problems in Public Policy: Understanding and Responding to Complex Challenges, p.176, Springer Nature.

that altering one thread invariably reshapes the whole tapestry.[79]

One of the most confounding aspects of a wicked problem is that you can rarely be certain you're even addressing the right issue. Clarity about cause and effect is elusive, and feedback often arrives muddled or too late to guide corrective action. In many cases, it isn't clear whether progress has been made.

Meanwhile, as you wrestle with imperfect information, the context around the problem shifts. New technologies emerge, stakeholder priorities evolve, and competitors or counterparts pursue their own agendas, all of which continually redraw the boundaries of what needs solving.

Wicked problems live in arenas of competing values. They demand negotiation among groups whose perspectives and goals often collide. No single leader or rulebook can dictate a solution, because no one person holds both the insight and the authority to command agreement across all parties.[80] Instead, progress comes through experimentation, coalition-building and adaptive learning.

In the face of such wickedness, security professionals must cultivate flexibility, foster inclusive dialogue and embrace iterative approaches, recognising that each small gain may reveal new twists in the problem's shape, and that every solution must remain open to revision.

---

79 Wood, R.E., 1986, 'Task complexity: Definition of the construct', Organizational Behavior and Human Decision Processes, 37(1), pp.60–82.

80 Weber, M., 1978, Economy and Society: An Outline of Interpretive Sociology (Vol. 1), University of California Press.

Security professionals must learn to recognise a wicked problem when they see one, resisting the natural impulse to dictate precise solutions. They need patience, persistence and a tolerance for the ambiguity that comes with relinquishing full control. In the middle of uncertainty and conflict, they must remain resilient, modelling the kind of calm inquiry they wish to foster in their teams.

One cannot apply traditional methods to solving a wicked problem. Security professionals must instead probe, sense and respond to create experiments that allow patterns to emerge. They should increase levels of communication, particularly across boundaries, involving stakeholders from diverse fields.[81]

A creative solution must be sought. One of these could be to apply *design thinking* techniques.

Design thinking methodology established at d.school at Standford University offers a powerful, human-centred framework for tackling the complex challenges of information security by deeply understanding how people behave, make decisions and interact with technology.

At its core, design thinking is an iterative process, alternating between expanding our view to discover people's needs in context and narrowing our focus to develop, prototype and test solutions that fit those needs.

Originating in the design world, this approach has been embraced by businesses as a way to reframe strategic

---

[81] Snowden, D.J. and Boone, M.E., 2007, 'A leader's framework for decision making', Harvard Business Review, 85(11), p.68.

problems, generate creative ideas and build innovations that deliver real value.

In information security, this means observing how people respond to security controls, ideating ways to make safe behaviours more natural, rapidly prototyping features – such as simplified authentication flows or contextual phishing alerts – and testing them with real people.

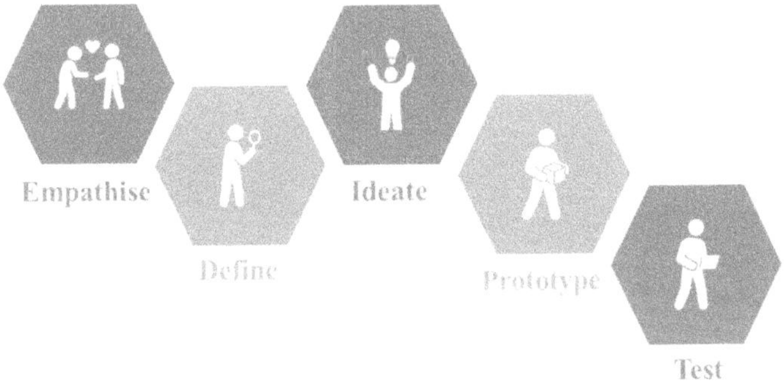

Figure 16: d.school design thinking methodology

By cycling through empathy, definition, ideation, prototyping and testing, each time converging on clearer problem statements and more refined solutions, security professionals can create security mechanisms that people understand, trust and willingly adopt, transforming 'secure by design' from a slogan into everyday reality.

There are four rules to design thinking, which can help security professionals better approach wicked problems[82]:

1. The human rule: all design activity is ultimately social in nature.
2. The ambiguity rule: design thinkers must preserve ambiguity.
3. The redesign rule: all design is redesign.
4. The tangibility rule: making ideas tangible always facilitates communication.

Security professionals should adopt these rules to develop secure and usable controls, by engaging people and allowing for feedback collection.

The *lean startup* process[83] complements the design thinking approach and brings a scientific, hypothesis-driven methodology to innovation that is equally valuable in information security.

---

[82] Plattner, H., Meinel, C. and Leifer, L. J. (eds.), 2010, Design thinking: understand–improve–apply, Springer Science & Business Media.
[83] Reis, E., 2011, 'The lean startup', New York: Crown Business, 27, pp.2016–2020.

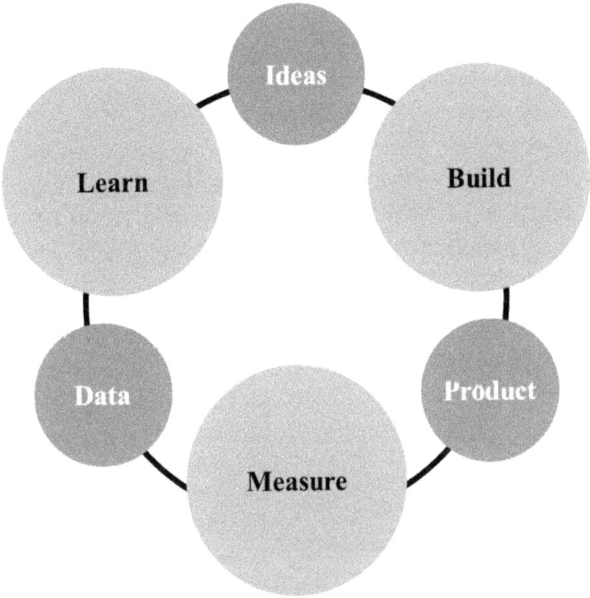

Figure 17: The lean startup process[84]

Rather than investing heavily in untested tools, security professionals can begin by articulating their most critical assumption about what will change people's behaviour to reduce risk.

For example, a team might hypothesise that employees delay updates because they lack clear, real-time visibility into their device's patch status.

Next, the team rapidly builds a minimum viable product: a simple prototype with just enough functionality to test the

---

[84] Reis, E., 2011, 'The lean startup', New York: Crown Business, 27, pp.2016–2020.

hypothesis in the real world. For instance, they create a minimal plugin that adds a simple red, amber or green icon signalling each workstation's patch health. They deploy it to a pilot group rather than redesigning the entire system. By focusing on the smallest experiment that can validate or invalidate the core assumption, security professionals conserve resources and gain early insight into people's behaviour.

In the measure phase, data (e.g. percentage of machines moving from red to green within 24 hours of the badge appearing) and qualitative feedback (e.g. via the one-click "Was this helpful?" prompt) are collected to assess whether the prototype meets expectations.

If employees take action as intended and provide positive feedback, the team learns that the hypothesis holds and can refine the design or tackle the next assumption. If, instead, adoption is low or people express confusion, the security professional treats this 'failure' as valuable learning: they can either pivot, reframing the problem, or abandon the approach and explore a different solution.

By cycling through Build–Measure–Learn in short iterations, security professionals adopt a human-centred, data-driven approach towards complex problems.

Whether developing new security tooling integrations, streamlining incident report dialogues or reimagining access-request workflows, applying lean startup enables every change to be grounded in real-world validation before scaling, maximising security outcomes while minimising wasted effort.

Security professionals gather early evidence about what drives behaviour and refine their approach based on data, incrementally building security mechanisms that people embrace.

***

Although this enables the design of better security controls, the design thinking or lean startup approaches rarely provide insight into why the existing mechanism is failing.

When a problem occurs, we naturally tend to focus on the symptoms instead of identifying the root cause. To get to the heart of the problem, the *Five Whys* technique, which was used in the Toyota production system, can be an invaluable systematic problem-solving tool. In this example, this technique was applied when a factory machine stopped functioning[85]:

1. Why did the machine stop? There was an overload and the fuse blew.
2. Why was there an overload? The bearing was not sufficiently lubricated.
3. Why was it not lubricated sufficiently? The lubrication pump was not pumping sufficiently.
4. Why was it not pumping sufficiently? The shaft of the pump was worn and rattling.

---

[85] Ohno, T., 1988, Toyota production system: beyond large-scale production, Productivity Press.

5. Why was the shaft worn out? There was no strainer attached and metal scrap got in.

Instead of focusing on resolving the first reason for the malfunction – replacing the fuse or the pump shaft – repeating “why” five (or more) times can help uncover the underlying issue and prevent the problem from resurfacing.

At “the root of every seemingly technical problem is actually a human problem”[86].

The root cause turned out to be human error (an employee forgetting to attach a strainer), rather than a technical fault (a blown fuse), as was initially suspected. This is typical of most problems that security professionals face, no matter which industry they are in.

Data suggests that the vast majority of data breaches can be attributed to ‘human error’[87].

But beyond the ‘human error’ is a deeper problem. While people do make mistakes, framing incidents this way often shuts down further analysis, discourages learning and undermines a culture of shared responsibility.

Not every error is a deliberate violation. Errors may occur due to unintended skill-related slips and lapses as well as knowledge and rule-based mistakes. These call for different interventions, such as better interface design for slips, checklists and reminders for lapses, decision aids and

---

[86] Reis, E., 2011, The lean startup, Crown Business.
[87] UK Information Commissioner’s Office (ICO), 2025, ‘Data security incident trends’.

training for mistakes, and policy design and enforcement for violations[88,89].

Instead of blaming individuals, security professionals should recognise these incidents as breakdowns in the system – signals that something in the processes, environment or design needs improvement. They should aim to uncover organisational, technical and cognitive factors that allowed the error, rather than assuming malice or negligence.[90]

People's behaviour emerges from the structure of the system in which they operate. Security professionals must strive to address the core of the issue and build systems that are both usable and secure.

Systems thinking[91] is a discipline that can help security professionals improve their ability to see the bigger picture and move beyond simplistic linear cause–effect relationships and point-in-time snapshots. It's a mindset that encourages security professionals to see interdependencies, processes and patterns of complex systems.

---

[88] Reason, J., 1990, Human Error, Cambridge University Press.
[89] Rasmussen, J., 2012, 'Skills, rules, and knowledge; signals, signs, and symbols, and other distinctions in human performance models', IEEE Transactions on Systems, Man, and Cybernetics, (3), pp.257–266.
[90] Woods, D., Dekker, S., Cook, R., Johannesen, L. and Sarter, N., 2017, Behind Human Error, CRC Press.
[91] Meadows, D.H., 2008, Thinking in Systems: A Primer, Chelsea Green Publishing.

Complex systems are tangled webs of interacting feedback loops, which is exactly why they're so hard to understand, diagnose and fix. With practice, security professionals learn to spot the leverage points – small, well-placed changes that produce outsized shifts in system behaviour – and use them to steer the system towards safer outcomes.

Systems thinking can help reframe security: not as a barrier against 'human error', but as an adaptive network that co-creates safe practices. When we surface mental models, we design environments where compliance flows naturally, and risky behaviours diminish.

A security professional's greatest leverage lies in changing paradigms: shifting from "security is someone else's job" to "security is how we work together". This is the foundation for the culture of security.

CHAPTER 15: BUILDING A CULTURE OF SECURITY

When security culture is strong, people treat safeguarding information as a team effort woven into their everyday activities. In that environment, employees are quick to spot problems and offer improvements, boosting overall resilience. They feel safe reporting concerns without retaliation and are far less likely to rely on unsanctioned 'shadow IT'.

A supportive security culture fosters inclusion and clarity around why rules exist, enhancing staff wellbeing and retention. Without a positive security culture, employees disengage, hiding workarounds and leaving the organisation blind to risks and valuable insights.

Demonstrating to people that security is there to make their life easier, not harder, is the first step in developing a sound security culture.

An organisation's security culture encompasses the collective knowledge, beliefs, perceptions, attitudes and norms that employees hold about security – and how these translate into their everyday interactions with technology. It means weaving security practices into the fabric of each person's role and habits. When information security is approached correctly, a robust security culture emerges organically from employees' daily treatment of data and systems.[92] Because it is part of the broader organisational culture, security culture can be actively guided and reshaped over time.[93]

An organisation's ability to manage risk effectively depends heavily on the strength and alignment of its culture. Without a culture that genuinely supports and integrates risk management and security practices into everyday activities, even the most robust frameworks and well-documented policies will quickly lose their impact.

This culture informs not only how risks are perceived but also how seriously they are addressed. A weak or misaligned culture can undermine risk initiatives, override formal processes and lead to significant blind spots in security governance.

While culture often manifests implicitly, described colloquially as "the way we do things around here"[94], it plays a powerful role in shaping expectations around acceptable and unacceptable behaviour. In the context of security, this includes attitudes towards data protection, incident reporting and personal accountability.

---

[92] Martins, A. and Eloff, J., 2002, 'Information security culture', Proceedings of the IFIP TC11 17th International Conference on Information Security (SEC2002), Cairo, Egypt, pp. 203–214.

[93] Ross, S. J. and Masters, R., 2011, Creating a Culture of Security, Butterworth-Heinemann; Ngo, L., 2008, 'IT security culture transition process', MSc dissertation, Edith Cowan University, Perth, Australia.

[94] Deal, T. and Kennedy, A., 2000, Corporate Cultures: The Rites and Rituals of Corporate Life, Rev. edn, Basic Books, New York.

Culture can be understood at three interacting levels[95]:

1. The values an organisation embraces.
2. The behaviours people visibly adopt.
3. The deep-seated assumptions that guide thought.

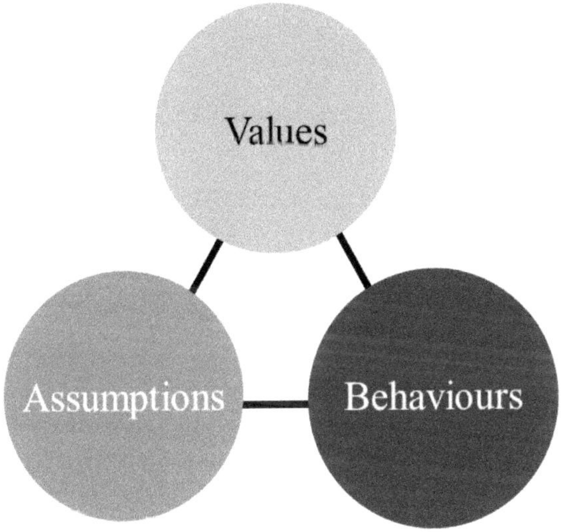

Figure 18: Organisational culture levels

Culture change begins by redefining values, which then drive new patterns of behaviour. When those behaviours prove effective, they become ingrained, eventually solidifying into the organisation's underlying assumptions.

---

[95] Schein, E.H., 1984, 'Coming to a new awareness of organizational culture', Sloan Management Review, 25(2), pp.3–16.

Security culture is not a standalone initiative. It must be integrated into the broader organisational culture, reinforcing the idea that managing security risks is not the sole responsibility of a dedicated team but a shared commitment across the organisation.

Culture extends beyond mere compliance by shifting the mindset from "Can we do this?" to "Should we do this?", introducing an ethical lens to decision-making.

This becomes particularly important in the information security context.

Security professionals must champion the ethical use of data to protect individual rights and privacy. They have a positive impact on society by ensuring lawfulness, fairness and transparency when it comes to handling people's data.

As a security professional, imagine you discovered a large volume of unsecured data in your organisation. There may be no reason to store this data, but the company could be holding on to it 'just in case' and it's too hard and expensive to secure it properly.

Some executives may suggest that everyone in the industry is doing this, and there may even be a chance they could monetise it in the future.

It's the role of a security professional to challenge organisations to consider the long-term perspective[96], not only the immediate revenue targets. What would be the impact on reputation and trust if customers found out?

---

[96] Gentile, M. C., 2017, 'Giving Voice to Values: A Brief Introduction', Darden Business Publishing, 22 February.

To tackle ethical dilemmas like this effectively, it's helpful to position yourself as an agent of continual improvement and suggest a workable alternative. For example, security professionals could help develop a process to securely destroy customer data after it's no longer needed.

Help the executives see the organisation's wider purpose: it's not just to make money, it's to do right by the customers and partners. Because not securing their information appropriately may lead to data breaches.

Security professionals can remind them that the effects on people whose personal data is misused can be devastating: their identity can be stolen, they can become victims of fraud and lose their money, their mental health can be affected. It's our responsibility to protect them.

Implementing an organisation-wide data protection strategy that is firmly grounded in ethics and values can result in a significant reduction in potential harm to people in the event of a data breach.

A stark example of culture gone wrong unfolded after two fatal crashes of Boeing's 737 Max aircraft: in Indonesia in October 2018 and in Ethiopia just 19 weeks later. Since its founding in 1916, Boeing had built a reputation on quality, teamwork, innovation and 'safety first', fostering deep pride and belonging among its workforce. But after merging with McDonnell Douglas in 1997, Boeing shifted its focus towards shareholder returns. Massive restructuring and cost-cutting measures streamlined production at the expense of rigorous safety standards. Employees were urged to prioritise profits, and bad news about potential design or manufacturing problems was quietly buried rather than raised.

Investigations and a US Congressional inquiry revealed that both crashes were triggered by flaws in the new Manoeuvring Characteristics Augmentation System (MCAS), a sensor-driven feature that could force the plane's nose downward. Yet Boeing had kept MCAS's existence, and its need for pilot training, secret, even as it blamed the first disaster on pilot error. When the second crash exposed the underlying design failures, it became painfully clear that Boeing had sacrificed transparency and accountability in pursuit of financial targets. The fallout was devastating: the global grounding of the 737 Max fleet for nearly two years, crippling reputational harm, lost sales, hefty fines and lawsuits from victims' families.[97]

Executives may not have meant to foster toxic environments, but collective complacency and overconfidence allowed poor values to take root. The long-term economic toll of such cultural failures, including regulatory penalties, talent loss and irreversible damage to brand trust, far outweighs any short-term gains.

This speaks directly to the root cause of poor culture: bad habits and behaviours tend to be contagious and "spread like viruses".[98]

The *broken windows theory* illustrates the power of context.[99] This advocates for stopping smaller crimes by maintaining the environment to prevent bigger ones. The

---

[97] Kennedy, R., 2022, Downfall: The case against Boeing [Film].

[98] Gladwell, M., 2006, The tipping point: how little things can make a big difference, Little, Brown.

[99] Wilson, J. Q. and Kelling, G. L., 1982, 'Broken windows: the police and neighborhood safety', The Atlantic, 29(31), pp. 29–38.

authors claim that a broken window left for several days in a neighbourhood would trigger more vandalism. The small defect signals a lack of care and attention, which in turn implies that crime will go unpunished.

George Kelling employed the theory to fight vandalism on the New York City subway system. He argued that cleaning up graffiti on the trains would prevent further vandalism and more severe crimes. It was concluded that this several-years-long effort resulted in a dramatically reduced crime rate.

Despite ongoing debate regarding the causes of the 1990s crime rate reduction in the US, the broken windows theory can be applied in the information security context.

Security professionals should remember that minor policy violations like reusing passwords or skipping patches tend to create easy footholds for attackers and can lead to actions that significantly increase organisational cyber risk, eroding the security culture.

If staff frequently disregard security policies, those behaviours act like 'broken windows', telling everyone that security isn't taken seriously. Address this by encouraging staff to report any security concerns, even minor ones, and act on small infractions quickly to demonstrate that security matters throughout the organisation.

***

We discussed the common reasons for violations in Chapter 11, but there is more to the story. The psychology of human behaviour should also be considered. Often, people are not motivated to comply with a security policy because they simply don't see the immediate and direct impact of violating it.

We can draw parallels with cheating. In one experiment, golf players were surveyed to determine the conditions in which they would be tempted to move the ball into a more advantageous position, and if so, which method they would choose.[100] The golfers were offered three different options: they could use their club, use their shoe or pick the ball up using their hands.

Although all of these options break the rules, they were designed to determine if one method of cheating was more psychologically acceptable than others. The results of the study demonstrated that moving the ball with a club was the most common choice, followed by the shoe and, finally, the hand. It turned out that physically and psychologically distancing ourselves from the 'immoral' action makes people more likely to act dishonestly. The 'distance' described in this experiment is merely psychological; it doesn't change the nature of the action.

In the security context, employees will usually be reluctant to steal confidential information, just as golfers will refrain from picking up a ball with their hand to move it to a more favourable position, because that way they are directly involved in the unethical behaviour. However, employees may break security policy in minor ways – like using unsanctioned software or services – as the impact of these actions is less obvious. This can potentially lead to even

[100] Ariely, D. 2013, The honest truth about dishonesty. Harper.

bigger losses due to more confidential information being exposed through excessive permissions, misconfiguration or malware-related exfiltration.

Security professionals can use this finding to remind employees of the true meaning of their actions. Breaking security policy does not seem to have a direct financial impact on the organisation – there is usually no perceived loss – so it is easy for employees to engage in such behaviour. Highlighting this link and demonstrating the correlation between policy violations and the organisation's ability to generate revenue or deliver on its mission could help employees understand the consequences of insecure practices.

Building upon the connection between breaking security policies and cheating, let's look at another study. Participants had to solve a number of simple maths problems and were promised a small monetary reward for each correct answer.[101]

They were allowed to check their own answers and then shred the answer sheet, leaving no evidence of any potential cheating. The results demonstrated that participants reported solving on average five more problems than under conditions where cheating was not possible (i.e. controlled conditions).

The researchers then introduced David, a student who was tasked to raise his hand shortly after the experiment began and proclaim that he had solved all the problems. Other

---

[101] Gino, F., Ayal, S. and Ariely, D., 2009, 'Contagion and differentiation in unethical behavior: the effect of one bad apple on the barrel', Psychological Science, 20(3), pp. 393–398.

participants were, of course, shocked. It was clearly impossible to solve all the problems in only a few minutes. The experimenter, however, didn't question his integrity and suggested that David should shred the answer sheet and take all the money from the envelope.

Interestingly, other participants' behaviour adapted as a result. They reported solving on average eight more problems than under controlled conditions.

Much like the broken windows theory, this demonstrates that unethical behaviour is as contagious as insecure practices. If employees witness other people breaking security policies with no consequences, they are tempted to do the same; it becomes socially acceptable. This is the root cause of poor security culture.

The good news is that the opposite holds true. That's why security culture must have strong senior management support. Leading by example is the key to changing the perception of security: if employees see that the leadership team takes security seriously, they will follow.

People are inherently social and tend to follow the norms of their group. Because individuals seek approval, they often adjust their actions to match what they believe managers and colleagues expect. When leadership visibly prioritises security, it creates powerful social signals that drive others to comply.

Employees become even more committed to security measures when they see their peers doing the same.[102] People's natural tendency to imitate others, especially in unfamiliar situations, is one of the strongest catalysts for changing behaviour.[103] Therefore, security professionals should focus on how security is perceived to achieve lasting behavioural change.

---

[102] Herath, T. and Rao, H.R., 2009, 'Encouraging information security behaviors in organizations: Role of penalties, pressures and perceived effectiveness', Decision Support Systems, 47(2), pp.154–165.

[103] Cialdini, R.B. and Goldstein, N.J., 2004, 'Social Influence: Compliance and Conformity', Annual Review of Psychology, 55(1), pp.591–621.

CHAPTER 16: THE PSYCHOLOGY OF BEHAVIOURAL CHANGE

The three basic steps in decision-making are[104]:

1. People perceive a situation;
2. People estimate if the action is in their long-term interest; and
3. People use willpower to take action.

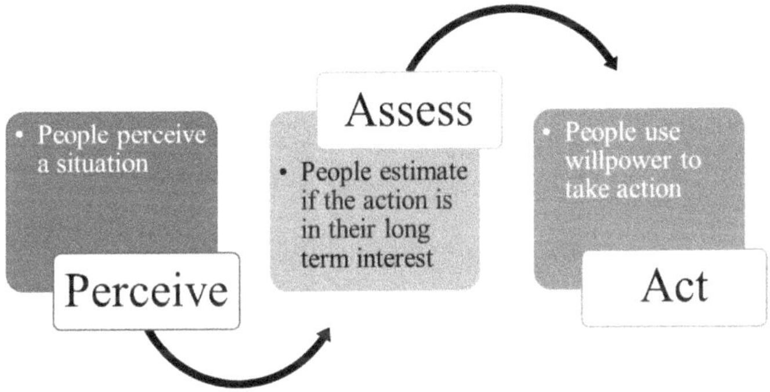

Figure 19: Basic steps of decision-making

To change behaviour, people historically were mostly focused on the last two steps of this process. However, Chapter 13 demonstrated that relying on willpower alone has a limited effect. Willpower can be exercised like a muscle, but it is also prone to atrophy.

---

[104] Brooks, D., 2011, The social animal: The hidden sources of love, character, and achievement. Random House.

As for the second step of the decision-making process, if people were reminded of the potential negative consequences, they would likely not take the action. However, the ineffective HIV/AIDS awareness campaigns, which focused only on the negative consequences, ultimately failed to change people's behaviour.[105]

Most diets fail because willpower and reason alone are not strong enough to confront impulsive desires. "You can tell people not to eat the French fry. You can give them pamphlets about the risks of obesity … In their nonhungry state, most people will vow not to eat it. But when their hungry self rises, their well-intentioned self fades, and they eat the French fry."[106]

This doesn't only apply to dieting. As demonstrated in Chapter 9, when people want to get their job done and security gets in the way, they will circumvent it, regardless of the degree of risk they might expose the organisation to.

That is the reason for perception being the cornerstone of the decision-making process. Employees need to be guided to see unsafe behaviour in a particular way that minimises the temptation to engage in actions that increase organisational cyber risk.

"One of the most enduring lessons of social psychology is that behaviour change often precedes changes in attitudes and feelings."[107]

---

[105] Ibid.

[106] Brooks, D., 2011, The social animal: The hidden sources of love, character, and achievement. Random House.

[107] Wilson, T., 2004, Strangers to ourselves, Harvard University Press.

There is no single event that alters people's behaviour – changing security culture requires regular reinforcement, creating and sustaining habits.

Lasting habits stem from identity: we repeat behaviours that reinforce our self-image. "Every action is a vote for the type of person you want to become."[108]

Security professionals can help cultivate a collective identity, like "we are a trustworthy organisation that protects our customers' data".

When employees see themselves as guardians of trust, secure behaviours become intrinsically motivating rather than chores.

Consider the story of Paul O'Neill, CEO of the Aluminum Company of America (Alcoa).[109] He was determined to make his organisation the safest in the country. At first, people were confused that the newly appointed executive was not talking about profit margins or other finance-related metrics. They didn't see the link between his "zero-injuries" goal and the organisation's performance. Despite that, Alcoa's profits reached a historical high within a year of his announcement. When O'Neill retired, Alcoa's annual income was five times greater than it had been before his arrival. It also became one of the safest organisations in the world.

---

[108] Clear, J., 2018, Atomic habits: Tiny changes, remarkable results, Penguin Publishing Group.

[109] Duhigg, C., 2013, The Power of Habit: Why We Do What We Do and How to Change, Random House.

O'Neill had a challenging goal to transform Alcoa, but he couldn't just tell people to change their behaviour. He said, "that's not how the brain works. So I decided I was going to start by focusing on one thing. If I could start disrupting the habits around one thing, it would spread throughout the entire company."

He identified safety as such a "keystone habit" and focused solely on it.

O'Neill recalled an incident when one of his workers died trying to fix a machine despite the safety procedures and warning signs. The CEO called an emergency meeting to understand what had caused this tragic event.

He took personal responsibility for the worker's death, identifying numerous shortcomings in safety education. For example, the training programme didn't highlight the fact that employees wouldn't be blamed for machinery failure or that they shouldn't commence repair work before finding a manager.

As a result, the policies were updated, and employees were encouraged to suggest safety improvements. Workers, however, went a step further by suggesting business improvements. Changing their behaviour around safety led to innovative solutions, enhanced communication and increased profits.

Learning from our mistakes and the mistakes of others is crucial if we want to improve. One key psychological obstacle is cognitive dissonance: when evidence contradicts our beliefs, we're more likely to twist the facts than change our views.[110]

Security is no exception. Security professionals should understand the importance of such influences and group dynamics to build an effective security culture where feedback is honestly assessed and used to drive improvement.

Just as 'broken windows' encourages policy violations, changing one security habit can encourage more productive behaviour across the board.

Security culture can build on safety culture: many organisations in the critical infrastructure sector adopt a 'zero injuries' goal where they strive towards minimising safety incidents. An aspirational 'zero security breaches' goal can complement that.

This doesn't mean all security incidents get prevented; rather, staff are encouraged to detect, report and act on them. People learn from incidents and address the root causes to stop them from reoccurring.

For example, a pre-mortem technique can be used where a team begins with imagining a security incident occurring and works backwards to potential flaws that might have led to it, thus identifying and implementing risk mitigation measures before an incident occurs.

Just like with safety, every person in the organisation has a responsibility and role to play. The same safety protocols are often applied on both the factory floor and in the office:

---

[110] Syed, M., 2015, Black Box Thinking: Why Most People Never Learn from Their Mistakes-But Some Do, Penguin.

people will actively intervene and tell you off if you are not holding the handrail while going down the stairs or carrying a cup of coffee without a lid. It's part of the culture.

To be effective, cyber security needs to build on and plug into these safety protocols. In traditional IT environments, confidentiality is often prioritised. In critical infrastructure, safety and availability are paramount.

Changing the mindset and adopting safety-related principles (like ALARP: as low as reasonably practicable[111]) and methods (like Bowtie[112] to visualise cause and consequence relationships in incident scenarios) when managing risk is a step in the right direction.

Small, consistent changes are more effective than one-off goals. By repeatedly choosing the same secure behaviour in response to common scenarios, people's brains make that response the default, reducing both stress and the mental effort required to make the right security decisions.

***

---

[111] Jones-Lee, M. and Aven, T., 2011, 'ALARP — what does it really mean?', Reliability Engineering & System Safety, 96(8), pp. 877–882.

[112] de Ruijter, A. and Guldenmund, F., 2016, 'The bowtie method: A review', Safety Science, 88, pp.211–218.

Behaviour arises from the interaction of individual and environment.[113] Changing one without the other limits impact.

The COM-B model[114], as shown in Figure 20, is particularly applicable in the security context to gain insight into the causes of unsafe behaviour and design interventions.

The model suggests that secure behaviour, such as locking your screen before you leave your desk, only occurs when three conditions are met: *capability* (you know how to do it), *opportunity* (you have the means and time to do it) and *motivation* (you want to do it).

---

[113] Lewin, K., 2013, Principles of Topological Psychology, Read Books Ltd.

[114] Michie, S., Van Stralen, M.M. and West, R., 2011, 'The behaviour change wheel: a new method for characterising and designing behaviour change interventions', Implementation Science, 6, pp.1–12.

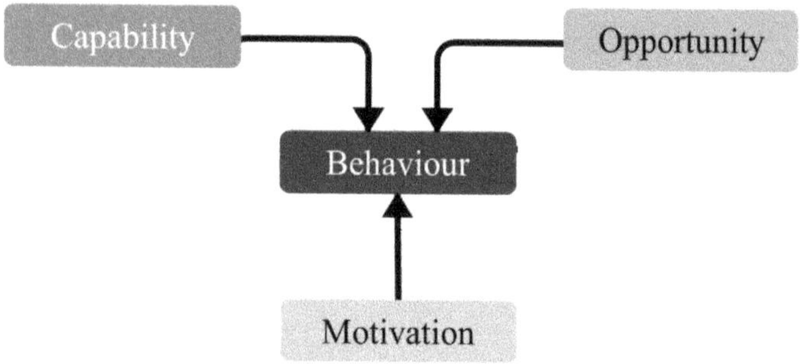

Figure 20: COM-B model[115]

Which lever you pull depends on which element is missing. If people can lock their screens and have the chance to do so, but simply aren't motivated, then security professionals need interventions that boost motivation – through awareness campaigns, incentives or policy enforcement. Conversely, if motivation is high but people lack the know-how (capability), you focus on training and skills development.[116]

Importantly, security professionals must diagnose the real barrier. Some employees admit they both know how and understand the need to lock their screens yet avoid it

[115] Adapted from Michie, S., Van Stralen, M. M. and West, R., 2011, 'The behaviour change wheel: a new method for characterising and designing behaviour change interventions', Implementation Science, 6, pp. 1–12.
[116] ENISA, 2018, 'Cyber Security Culture in organisations'.

because it feels like a vote of no-confidence in colleagues' trustworthiness.[117]

The solution, therefore, shouldn't be another tutorial but an educational shift: staff need to see screen locking as an organisational security habit, not a personal slight. Once people understand that their peers view it as part of normal business practice, the perceived trust issue goes away, and the behavioural blocker is removed.

This distinction between real-world trust and online trust also underpins effective security education.[118] Social engineering attacks prey on our instinct to trust familiar cues. Employees must learn when and how to verify identities online, by consulting security teams, using secondary channels for confirmation or politely declining suspicious requests.

Ultimately, empowering staff with the right understanding and skills lets them act confidently so that, when faced with a genuine threat, they can proudly say, "I stopped that attack."

---

[117] Kirlappos, I., Parkin, S., Sasse, M.A., 2015, 'Shadow security as a tool for the learning organization', ACM SIGCAS Computers and Society, 45(1), pp.29–37, doi:10.1145/2738210.2738216.

[118] Sasse, M.A. and Kirlappos, I., 2014, 'Design for Trusted and Trustworthy Services: Why We Must Do Better', Trust, Computing, and Society, pp.229–249.

A related model, the Fogg Behaviour Model, suggests that *behaviour* occurs when *motivation*, *ability* and a *prompt* converge simultaneously.[119]

In other words, even if employees want to follow security policies, they will only do so when they *can* easily comply and are *prompted* to act.

For example, an employee highly motivated to secure their account will still choose not to enable MFA if they don't know how (low ability) or aren't given a cue to do so (missing prompt).

In practical terms, this means every secure behaviour in the workplace, from reporting a phishing email to applying software patches, depends on all three factors being addressed. If any one is missing, the safe behaviour has a higher chance of failing.

Let's explore these factors in more detail.

1. *Motivation* is the employee's desire or reason to perform a secure behaviour, supported by three core drives: sensation, anticipation and belonging. Security professionals can tap into these drives by aligning desired behaviours with what people already want, e.g. convenience of single sign-on, recognition through leadership support or vision of success: "you're protecting the entire organisation when you report phishing emails".
2. *Ability* refers to how easy it is for an employee to perform the security behaviour. The key factors

---

[119] Fogg, B.J., 2019, Fogg Behavior Model, Behaviour Design Lab, Stanford University, Stanford, CA, USA, Tech. Rep.

include time, physical effort, mental effort, deviation from routine or social norms involved in an action.

In security contexts, these translate into the common barriers that make secure practices feel onerous. For instance, complex security protocols that consume a lot of time or attention will translate into low ability for busy staff.

To counter this, security professionals should automate or simplify tasks where possible to reduce friction. Rather than relying solely on training, they should provide resources to make the behaviour easier. Like in the Alcoa example earlier, they must scale back and focus on a single habit, rather than implementing complex initiatives across multiple domains.

Security professionals should design mechanisms that do the hard work for people. For example, reducing the reliance on passwords or providing a company password manager offloads the cognitive load of creating and remembering strong passwords. Similarly, enabling single sign-on, automatic software updates and email scanning reduces the mental effort.

Security professionals must also avoid technical jargon and long procedures in policies. Instead, they should give clear, easy instructions. People can't act on a message if they don't understand it.

3. A *prompt* is a reminder to perform the desired behaviour. These need to be clear, contextual and timely, delivered in the moment they are needed and state the desired action, e.g. "install update now".

Prompts should be designed based on people's motivation and ability. If these factors are low, people won't act, even if prompted.

A holistic approach to behaviour change is needed for the interplay between factors: if security professionals can't raise employee motivation, they may strive to make the task easier and vice versa.

Applied consistently, an approach based on the Fogg Behaviour Model can significantly improve real-world security behaviours. For instance, one study designed a prompt for smartphone users based on the model and achieved a significant increase in adoption of recommended security practices.[120] In this study, tailored mobile prompts, aligned with people's motivations and made easy to follow, outperformed standard training.

Another way to describe prompts is *nudges*. A good complement to the Fogg Behaviour Model is the nudge theory.

We discussed human biases, heuristics and the complexity of decision-making earlier in the book; the nudge theory is strongly influenced by these concepts.

Rather than making purely rational decisions, humans make decisions that may not be optimal but are 'good

---

[120] Shah, P.R., 2024, November, 'Fogg Behavioural Model Based Cybersecurity Awareness Framework: An Empirical Analysis', in Indian Conference on Human-Computer Interaction Design and Research (pp.51–69), Cham: Springer Nature Switzerland.

enough' given the time, uncertainty and cognitive constraints.[121]

Human decision-making can be enriched by improving the environment in which decisions are made, giving people more time and resources and providing feedback on their decisions.[122]

Nudges can help steer the decisions while preserving the freedom of choice by changing the choice architecture: the context in which people make decisions.[123] Nudges, therefore, become features of the environment that influence decisions: restaurant menus, website designs, store layouts, etc.

Security professionals can take these features of the environment and adjust them in a way that helps people make safer decisions.

For instance, security applications for nudges may range from default settings (e.g. having encryption and auto-update features enabled by default) and feedback cues (e.g. password strength meters) to social norms (e.g. "92% of your peers use MFA").

---

[121] Simon, H.A., 1990, 'Bounded rationality', Utility and Probability, pp.15–18.
[122] Kahneman, D. and Klein, G., 2009, 'Conditions for intuitive expertise: a failure to disagree', American Psychologist, 64(6), p.515.
[123] Thaler, R.H. and Sunstein, C.R., 2021, Nudge: The Final Edition, Penguin.

Such security nudges have been applied to improve phishing email detection[124], decisions about installing privacy-invasive mobile apps[125], social media sharing[126] and smartphone privacy settings.[127]

Researchers also applied simple nudges to increase voluntary e-learning module uptake.[128] They discovered that pairing transparent, moral-framing nudges with expert credibility effectively motivates engagement in optional, no-direct-reward training.

---

[124] Nicholson, J., Coventry, L. and Briggs, P., 2017, 'Can we fight social engineering attacks by social means? Assessing social salience as a means to improve phish detection', Proceedings of the 13th Symposium on Usable Privacy and Security (SOUPS 2017), Usenix, 12 July, pp. 787–796.

[125] Choe, E.K., Jung, J., Lee, B. and Fisher, K., 2013, 'Nudging People Away from Privacy-Invasive Mobile Apps through Visual Framing', Springer Berlin Heidelberg, pp.74–91.

[126] Wang, Y., Leon, P. G., Acquisti, A., Cranor, L. F., Forget, A. and Sadeh, N., 2014, 'A field trial of privacy nudges for Facebook', Proceedings of the 32nd Annual ACM Conference on Human Factors in Computing Systems (CHI '14), New York, NY, USA, pp. 2367–2376.

[127] lmuhimedi, H., Schaub, F., Sadeh, N., Adjerid, I., Acquisti, A., Gluck, J., Cranor, L.F. and Agarwal, Y., 2015, 'Your Location has been Shared 5,398 Times!', proceedings of the 33rd Annual ACM Conference on Human Factors in Computing Systems – CHI '15, New York, New York, USA, 2015, pp.787–796.

[128] Chohan, A., Bicknell, A. and Psychol, C., 2019, 'Applying nudge to organisational communications: nudge and source impact on e-learning completion', Contemporary Ergonomics and Human Factors.

By aligning message content (moral and social benefits) with a trusted messenger, security professionals can overcome inertia, foster a learning culture and drive higher adoption of critical security behaviours.

Nudges may build on known biases: loss aversion, anchoring, social conformity and commitment effects to guide people to more secure options by making these choices the path of least resistance while maintaining the freedom and transparency, something we discussed in Chapter 13.

Overall, nudges are a relatively inexpensive and scalable way to improve people's behaviour, with plenty of established nudging programmes across the private sector and government. However, they assume a positive intent by the nudger and a relatively high motivation of a nudgee.

To overcome some of these limitations, security professionals can employ a complementary approach to nudging: *boosting*. Rather than changing the choice architecture, boosting aims to improve people's ability to make decisions by targeting their skills and knowledge.[129]

While nudges can yield quick wins, they may falter when contexts change or when people disengage from externally imposed cues. Boosting, by contrast, fosters durable competence: employees learn how and why secure choices matter and how to embed prompts in their own workflows.

---

[129] Hertwig, R. and Grüne-Yanoff, T., 2017, 'Nudging and boosting: Steering or empowering good decisions', Perspectives on Psychological Science, 12(6), pp.973–986.

Security professionals can 'boost' people's competence to 'self-nudge' and make their own decisions. This transforms employees from passive recipients of prompts into active architects of their own security habits.

For example, a simple communication of risks and benefits has proven to change people's behaviour for the better. A study demonstrated that informative posters increased hand hygiene in a Dutch hospital by 20%.[130] Another study showed that 'boost' training can decrease mathematical misconception in adults.[131] It was also proven that educational boosts promoted choice-consistent effects on attitudes, intentions and knowledge.[132]

Security professionals can leverage boosting strategies for targeted educational campaigns, tailored to specific behaviours and stakeholder needs, to deepen people's security competence and autonomy.

---

[130] Van Roekel, H., Reinhard, J. and Grimmelikhuijsen, S., 2022, 'Improving hand hygiene in hospitals: comparing the effect of a nudge and a boost on protocol compliance', Behavioural Public Policy, 6(1), pp.52–74.

[131] Thompson, C.A., Taber, J.M., Sidney, P.G., Fitzsimmons, C.J., Mielicki, M.K., Matthews, P.G., Schemmel, E.A., Simonovic, N., Foust, J.L., Aurora, P. and Disabato, D.J., 2021, 'Math matters: A novel, brief educational intervention decreases whole number bias when reasoning about COVID-19', Journal of Experimental Psychology: Applied, 27(4), p.632.

[132] Tanner, B., Cokely, E.T. and Feltz, A., 2025, 'Defaults change choices, not minds: Practical and ethical benefits of brief educational boosts for water recycling acceptance', Judgment and Decision Making, 20, p.30.

Boosting may take longer to implement compared to nudges, but it offers a supporting, rather than competing, approach to behavioural change.

Focusing on systems rather than one-off goals, harnessing aggregation of marginal gains, embedding an identity of security and trust, and redesigning environments to match individual capabilities create a self-reinforcing culture of security. When every 'tiny habit' is made obvious, attractive, easy and satisfying[133], secure behaviour ceases to be an obstacle and becomes the organisation's natural rhythm.

---

[133] Clear, J., 2018, Atomic Habits: Tiny Changes, Remarkable Results, Penguin Publishing Group.

CHAPTER 17: EVOLVING THE APPROACH TO SECURITY

In 1899, Auguste Kerckhoffs set out six principles for a secure communications system, three of which emphasise the human element: keys should be easy to share and remember without written aids, the system must be portable, and so straightforward that people needn't struggle mentally or learn complex rules.[134]

Even the pioneers of cryptography recognised that true security depends on making security work smoothly for people.

Yet the focus remains on securing technology, while people are viewed as programmable parts, their actions governed by policies and enforced through technical controls or penalties.

Viewing people as mere components whose actions can be dictated by a handful of 'controls' is fundamentally flawed. Instead, employees and customers act as independent agents shaped by their own abilities and limits, guided by personal goals, norms and values.[135]

To reduce security risks within an organisation, security professionals have traditionally attempted to guide employee behaviour towards safety through security

---

[134] Petitcolas, F.A., 2025, 'Kerckhoffs' principle', Encyclopedia of Cryptography, Security and Privacy, pp.1342–1343, Cham: Springer Nature Switzerland.

[135] ENISA, 2018, 'Cybersecurity culture guidelines: behavioural aspects of cybersecurity'.

training. However, recurring problems and employee behaviour in this arena indicate that these measures are insufficient and rather ineffective.

Security training tends to focus on specific working practices and defined threat scenarios, leaving the understanding of security culture and its specific principles of behaviour untouched. A security culture should be regarded as a fundamental matter to address. If it is neglected, employees will not develop habitually secure behaviour or take the initiative to make better decisions when problems arise.

Behaviour change takes time and is unlikely to happen through a single campaign. It can only occur if desired secure behaviour is achievable in the context of an individual's everyday activities.

When information security mechanisms are created to fit into employees' day-to-day jobs, rates of compliance increase and a more positive outlook on security is attained, which in turn results in a healthier, stronger and more positive security culture.

If security professionals want to steer employee behaviour towards safety, they must first shift their decision-making processes in the same direction. To do so, security professionals must have a look at their individual cost-benefit analyses. Security implementations must not only accommodate people's needs and priorities but also be economically attractive.

There are three main factors that can help modify employee perception of the cost-benefit balance towards compliance: design, culture and monitoring.[136]

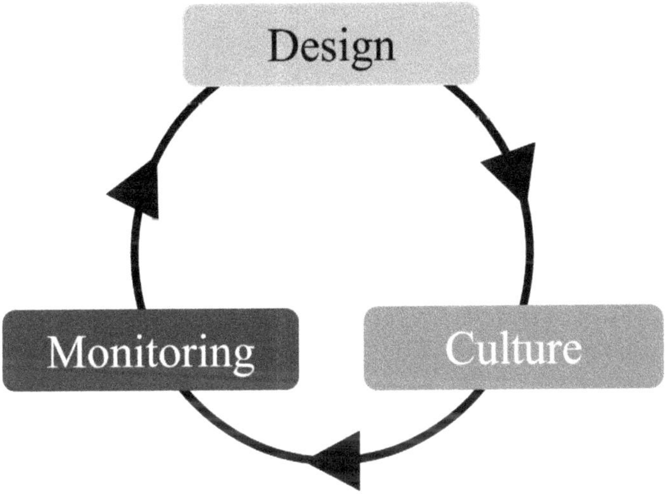

Figure 21: Factors that modify employee perception

Design

To minimise compliance costs, security professionals should make sure that security mechanisms are functioning properly within a specific context. For example, employees should be provided with encrypted laptop drives in case they have to store their documents locally, along with improved remote access that can diminish the need to

[136] Kirlappos, I., Beautement, A. and Sasse, M. A., 2013, ''Comply or die' is dead: long live security-aware principal agents', in Financial Cryptography and Data Security, Springer, pp. 70–82.

transfer information across different channels. Employees are less likely to reuse passwords if they are using passkeys, password managers and single sign-on systems.

Security professionals should facilitate the conditions that will enable situational and local adjustments to these security mechanisms. For example, when an employee needs to access a blocked website, they are given the option to proceed with the knowledge that activity will be logged and reviewed by the security team to ensure no malware was picked up.

This point focuses on the flexibility that employees may require to have access to certain systems to complete their primary tasks when they encounter a problem. Usually, when this occurs, they don't have the luxury of waiting for the authorised personnel to act and they will be forced to find workarounds to gain this access – they will normally resort to trusted work colleagues.

The security mechanisms, processes and technology must be closely aligned with the needs of the employees and the demands of their primary tasks.

Culture

Once employees' primary tasks are identified and aligned with the security systems that enable compliance, the next step is to create awareness of information risks and educate on the principles for managing them. The goal is not to teach tricks, but to create a culture that is accepted and understood by everyone.

Security professionals should regularly communicate how security fits into the broader organisational objectives, reinforcing that occasional friction is part of a larger safe operation.

To effectively do so, messages need to be designed and delivered according to each type of employee: there is no such thing as a one-size-fits-all security campaign. Questions that must always be answered include: What are the benefits? What does it matter or why should I care? What impact do my actions have?

Security awareness efforts must discard scare tactics such as threatening employees with sanctions for breaches; fear appeals have been proven ineffective in changing behaviour.[137] Campaigns should be oriented towards people's goals and values, as well as the values of the organisation, such as excellence and professionalism.

Security education should emphasise that employees can cause serious damage to an organisation when they engage in unsafe behaviour, even if it appears to be in an insignificant way. They should understand that they are bearing some responsibility for the security of the organisation and its exposure to cyber risk.

The entire organisation needs to perceive security as bringing value to the company, as opposed to being an obstacle preventing employees from doing their job. It is important for people to understand that they contribute to the smooth and efficient operation of business processes when they follow recommended security practices, just as

---

[137] Witte. K. and Allen, M., 2000, 'A meta-analysis of fear appeals: Implications for effective public health programs', Health Education and Behavior, 27(5), pp.591–615.

security enables the availability of resources that support these processes.

Security campaigns that are targeted enable greater flexibility: the more an organisation's employees are adequately aware of the need for security, the easier it is to create behavioural change through education. When everybody is sufficiently aware of the vulnerabilities and threats inherent in their jobs, the organisation can apply an effective training programme by testing their knowledge and then resort to education whenever a misconception is found.

From this point on, only role-specific reminders of the key messages are required to reinforce awareness and update employees on the latest risks. Easy-to-understand and engaging educational material and information should always be accessible to employees when they need a reference.

Monitoring

With appropriate design and culture, secure behaviour comes directly from employees who are interested in behaving securely and not as a result of the obstacles or threats imposed upon them. Voluntary safe behaviour is usually the result of standards that arise from both informal and formal rules within the organisation.

This method is significantly cheaper and easier to enforce, as it usually stems from, and further breeds, a positive atmosphere in which employees feel that their organisation trusts them to perform within compliance and even promote it. Organisations where employees have more responsibilities and feel trusted by their colleagues are more likely to establish a high level of security awareness and an improved understanding of the need for security.

However, if this trust is abused, monitoring and sanctioning mechanisms are required to prevent future transgressions.

* * *

If organisations continue to set equally high goals for both security and productivity, they are essentially leaving it up to their employees to resolve potential conflicts between them. As we have seen, employees focus most of their time and effort on carrying out their primary role effectively and in a timely manner, which means that their objective is to maximise their own benefit, as opposed to the organisation's.

It is therefore vital for organisations to find a balance between security and productivity, because when they fail to do so, they lead – or even force – their employees to resort to unsafe behaviour. When organisations are unable to recognise and correct security mechanisms and policies that affect performance and when they exclusively reward their employees for productivity, not for security, they are enabling and reinforcing insecure decision-making on behalf of the employees.

Employees will only comply with security policies if they are motivated to do so: they must have the perception that secure behaviour benefits them personally. People must be given the tools and the means to understand the risks associated with their roles, as well as the benefits of compliant behaviour, both to themselves and to the organisation. Once they are equipped with this information and awareness, they must be trusted to make their own decisions that can serve to mitigate risks at the organisational level.

The traditional approach, whereby security professionals 'police' employee performance by defining the security mechanisms without taking business processes or individual tasks into account, fails to work in modern distributed organisations that strive for agility and encourage individuals to take the initiative and make their ideas known.

Many organisations have evolved from compliance to risk-based information security frameworks, such as ISO 27001, but have not adapted their management of employees' security behaviour in the same way, which negatively influences employee compliance.

The rich diversity of the situational and local context, in which each person makes a decision, cannot be effectively or reasonably covered by a blanket approach. Flexibility and adaptability are key mechanisms to use when conflicts between security and business processes arise.

Security mechanisms must be aligned with individual primary tasks to achieve successful implementation, by factoring in an individual's perspective, knowledge and awareness in a modern, flexible and adaptable information security approach. The aim should therefore be to correct employee misunderstandings and misconceptions that result in unsafe practices, because, ultimately, people are an organisation's most important asset.

SOURCES

Acar, Y., Backes, M., Fahl, S., Kim, D., Mazurek, M. and Stransky, S., 2016, 'You get where you're looking for: The impact of information sources on code security', Proceedings of the 2016 IEEE Symposium on Security and Privacy (Oakland'16).

Adams, A. and Sasse, M.A., 1999, 'Users are not the enemy: Why users compromise security mechanisms and how to take remedial measures', Communications of the ACM, 42(12), pp. 40–46.

Adams, J., 2007, 'Risk management: It's not rocket science… it's much more complicated', Risk Management, 54(5), pp. 36–40.

Albrechtsen, E. and Hovden, J., 2009, 'The information security digital divide between information security managers and users', Computers & Security, 28(6), pp. 476–490.

Anttila, J. and Kajava, J., 2010, 'Challenging IS and ISM standardization for business benefits', Paper presented at ARES '10 International Conference on Availability, Reliability, and Security.

Ariely, D., 2013, 'The honest truth about dishonesty'. Harper.

Aytes, K. and Connolly, T., 2004, 'Computer and risky computing practices: A rational choice perspective', Journal of Organizational End User Computing, 16(2), pp. 22–40.

Bartsch, S. and Sasse, M.A., 2012, 'Guiding decisions on authorization policies: A participatory approach to decision support', ACM SAC 2012, Trento, Italy.

Bartsch, S. and Sasse, M.A., 2013, "How users bypass access control and why: The impact of authorization problems on individuals and the organization', ECIS 2013: The 21st European Conference in Information Systems.

Beautement, A., Sasse, M.A. and Wonham, M., 2008, 'The compliance budget: Managing security behaviour in organisations', Proceedings of the 2008 Workshop on New Security Paradigms (NSPW '08), pp. 47–58.

Björck, F., 2001, 'Security Scandinavian style'. PhD dissertation, Stockholm University.

Brooks, D., 2011, 'The social animal: The hidden sources of love, character, and achievement'. Random House.

Bulgurcu, B., Cavusoglu, H. and Benbasat, I., 2010, 'Information security policy compliance: An empirical study of rationality-based beliefs and information security awareness', MIS Quarterly, 34(3), pp. 523–548.

Carnegie, D., 2019, 'How to win friends and influence people'. Jaico Publishing House.

Choe, E.K., Jung, J., Lee, B. and Fisher, K., 2013, 'Nudging people away from privacy-invasive mobile apps through visual framing', Springer Berlin Heidelberg, pp. 74–91.

Chohan, A., Bicknell, A. and Psychol, C., 2019, 'Applying nudge to organisational communications: Nudge and source impact on e-learning completion', Contemporary Ergonomics and Human Factors.

Cialdini, R., 2001, 'Harnessing the science of persuasion', Harvard Business Review, October, pp. 72–79.

Cialdini, R.B. and Goldstein, N.J., 2004, 'Social influence: Compliance and conformity', Annual Review of Psychology, 55(1), pp. 591–621.

Clear, J., 2018, 'Atomic habits: Tiny changes, remarkable results'. Penguin Publishing Group.

Danziger, S., Levav, J. and Avnaim-Pesso, L., 2011, 'Extraneous factors in judicial decisions', Proceedings of the National Academy of Sciences, 108(17), pp. 6889–6892.

de Ruijter, A. and Guldenmund, F., 2016, 'The bowtie method: A review', Safety Science, 88, pp. 211–218.

Deal, T. and Kennedy, A., 2000, 'Corporate cultures: The rites and rituals of corporate life'. Rev. edn. New York: Basic Books.

Dhillon, G. and Backhouse, J., 2001, 'Current directions in IS security research: Towards socio-organizational perspectives', Information Systems Journal, 11(2), pp. 127–153.

D'Arcy, J., Hovav, A. and Galletta, D., 2009, 'User awareness of security countermeasures and its impact on information systems misuse: A deterrence approach', Information Systems Research, 17(1), pp. 79–98.

Duhigg, C., 2013, 'The Power of Habit: Why We Do What We Do and How to Change'. Random House.

Dweck, C.S., 2006, 'Mindset: The New Psychology of Success'. Random House.

ENISA, 2016, 'Smart hospitals: security and resilience for smart health service and infrastructures'.

ENISA, 2018a, 'Cybersecurity culture guidelines: behavioural aspects of cybersecurity'.

ENISA, 2018b, 'Cyber security culture in organisations'.

Etzioni, A., 2010, Moral dimension: toward a new economics, Simon and Schuster.

Fahl, A., Harbach, M., Perl, H., Kötter, M. and Smith, M., 2013, 'Rethinking SSL development in an appified world', Proceedings of the 2013 ACM Conference on Computer and Communications Security (CCS'13).

Finkelstein, S., Whitehead, J. and Campbell, A., 2008, Think again: why good leaders make bad decisions and how to keep it from happening to you, Harvard Business Press, Boston.

Fléchais, I., 2003, 'Bringing security home: a process for developing secure and usable systems', in ACM/SIGSAC New Security Paradigms Workshop, ACM, New York, NY, USA, pp. 49–57.

Fléchais, I., 2005, 'Designing secure and usable systems', PhD dissertation, University College London.

Fléchais, I., Riegelsberger, J. and Sasse, M. A., 2005, 'Divide and conquer: the role of trust and assurance in the design of secure socio-technical systems', in Proceedings of the 2005 Workshop on New Security Paradigms (NSPW '05), ACM, New York, NY, USA, pp. 33–41.

Floris, M. and Cuganesan, S., 2019, 'Project leaders in transition: manifestations of cognitive and emotional capacity', International Journal of Project Management, 37(3), pp. 517–532.

Fogg, B. J., 2019, Fogg Behavior Model, Behaviour Design Lab, Stanford University, Stanford, CA, USA, Tech. Rep.

Freeman, R. E. and McVea, J., 2001, 'A stakeholder approach to strategic management', Darden Business School Working Paper No. 01-02.

Friedman, B., Howe, D. C. and Felten, E., 2002, 'Informed consent in the Mozilla browser: implementing value-sensitive design', in System Sciences, HICSS, Proceedings of the 35th Annual Hawaii International Conference on System Sciences, IEEE.

Fulford, H. and Doherty, N. F., 2003, 'The application of information security policies in large UK-based organizations: an exploratory investigation', Information Management & Computer Security, 11(3), pp. 106–114.

Furnell, S. M., Jusoh, A. and Katsabas, D., 2006, 'The challenges of understanding and using security: a survey of end-users', Computers & Security, 25(1), pp. 27–35.

Garfinkel, S. L. and Shelat, A., 2003, 'Remembrance of data passed: a study of disk sanitization practices', IEEE Security & Privacy, 1, pp. 17–27.

Gentile, M. C., 2017, 'Giving voice to values: a brief introduction', Darden Business Publishing, 22 February.

Gino, F., Ayal, S. and Ariely, D., 2009, 'Contagion and differentiation in unethical behavior: the effect of one bad apple on the barrel', Psychological Science, 20(3), pp. 393–398.

Gladwell, M., 2006, 'The tipping point: how little things can make a big difference'. Little, Brown.

Goleman, D., 1998, Working with emotional intelligence. Bantam Books, New York.

Goleman, D., Boyatzis, R. and McKee, A., 2004, 'Primal leadership: learning to lead with emotional intelligence'. Harvard Business School Press, Boston.

Gordon, L. A. and Martin, P. L., n.d., 'Managing cybersecurity resources: a cost–benefit analysis'. McGraw-Hill.

Government Security Group, 2024, 'Improving security culture', UK Government.

Greenwald, S. J., Olthoff, K. G., Raskin, V. and Ruch, W., 2004, 'The user non-acceptance paradigm: INFOSEC's dirty little secret', Proceedings of the New Security Paradigms Workshop.

Hamel, G. and Prahalad, C. K., 1996, 'Competing for the future'. Harvard Business Press.

Hammond, J. S., Keeney, R. L. and Raiffa, H., 2006, 'The hidden traps in decision making', Harvard Business Review.

Happ, C., Melzer, A. and Steffgen, G., 2016, 'Trick with treat – reciprocity increases the willingness to communicate personal data', Computers in Human Behavior, 61, pp. 372–377.

Hemantha, S. B., Herath, C. and Herath, T., 2007, 'Cyber-insurance: copula pricing framework and implications for risk management', Proceedings of the Sixth Workshop on the Economics of Information Security, Carnegie Mellon University, 7–8 June.

Herath, T. and Rao, H. R., 2009, 'Encouraging information security behaviors in organizations: role of penalties, pressures and perceived effectiveness', Decision Support Systems, 47(2), pp. 154–165.

Herley, C., 2009, 'So long, and no thanks for the externalities: the rational rejection of security advice by users', in Proceedings of the 2009 Workshop on New Security Paradigms (NSPW '09), ACM, New York, NY, USA, pp. 133–144.

Herley, C., 2013, 'More is not the answer', IEEE Security & Privacy, 12(1), pp. 14–19.

Hertwig, R. and Grüne-Yanoff, T., 2017, 'Nudging and boosting: steering or empowering good decisions', Perspectives on Psychological Science, 12(6), pp. 973–986.

Herzberg, F., Mausner, B. and Snyderman, B. B., 1993, 'The motivation to work', new edn. Transaction.

Higgins, H. N., 1999, 'Corporate system security: towards an integrated management approach', Information Management and Computer Security, 7(5), pp. 217–222.

Ho, G., Mirian, A., Luo, E., Tong, K., Lee, E., Liu, L., Longhurst, C. A., Dameff, C., Savage, S. and Voelker, G. M., 2025, 'Understanding the efficacy of phishing training in practice', in 2025 IEEE Symposium on Security and Privacy (SP), pp. 37–54, IEEE.

Huang, D., Hu, Q. and Behara, R., 2006, 'Economics of information security investment in the case of simultaneous attacks', Proceedings of the Fifth Workshop on the Economics of Information Security, Cambridge University, 26–28 June.

Hughes, M., 2016, 'Leading changes: why transformation explanations fail', Leadership, 12(4), pp. 449–469.

Imuhimedi, H., Schaub, F., Sadeh, N., Adjerid, I., Acquisti, A., Gluck, J., Cranor, L. F. and Agarwal, Y., 2015, 'Your location has been shared 5,398 times!', Proceedings of the 33rd Annual ACM Conference on Human Factors in Computing Systems (CHI '15), New York, NY, USA, pp. 787–796.

Inglesant, P. G. and Sasse, M. A., 2010, 'The true cost of unusable password policies: password use in the wild', in Proceedings of the 28th International Conference on Human Factors in Computing Systems, Atlanta, GA: ACM, pp. 383–392.

International Organization for Standardization (ISO), 2009, ISO Guide 73:2009 Risk management — vocabulary, Geneva.

International Organization for Standardization (ISO), 2022a, ISO/IEC 27001:2022 Information security, cybersecurity and privacy protection — information security management systems — requirements, Geneva.

International Organization for Standardization (ISO), 2022b, ISO/IEC 27002:2022 Information security, cybersecurity and privacy protection — information security controls, Geneva.

James, H. L., 1996, 'Managing information systems security: a soft approach', in Proceedings of the 1996 Information Systems Conference of New Zealand (ISCNZ '96), IEEE Computer Society, Washington, DC.

Johnson, E. and Goetz, E., 2007, 'Embedding information security into the organisation', IEEE Security & Privacy, 3 (May–June), pp. 16–24.

Johnson, E. and Dynes, S., 2007, 'Inadvertent disclosure: information leaks in extended enterprise', Proceedings of the Sixth Workshop on the Economics of Information Security, Carnegie Mellon University, 7–8 June.

Jones-Lee, M. and Aven, T., 2011, 'ALARP — what does it really mean?', Reliability Engineering & System Safety, 96(8), pp. 877–882.

Kahneman, D. and Tversky, A., 1979, 'Prospect theory: an analysis of decision under risk', Econometrica, 47(2), pp. 263–291.

Kahneman, D. and Klein, G., 2009, 'Conditions for intuitive expertise: a failure to disagree', American Psychologist, 64(6), p. 515.

Kahneman, D., 2011, 'Thinking, fast and slow'. Penguin Books, London.

Lovallo, D. and Kahneman, D., 2003, 'Delusions of success: how optimism undermines executives' decisions', Harvard Business Review.

Karyda, M., Kiountouzis, E. and Kokolakis, S., 2005, 'Information systems security policies: a contextual perspective', Computers & Security, 24(3), pp. 246–260.

Kirlappos, I., Beautement, A. and Sasse, M. A., 2013, ''Comply or die' is dead: long live security-aware principal agents', in Financial Cryptography and Data Security, Springer, pp. 70–82.

Kirlappos, I. and Sasse, M. A., 2012, 'Security education against phishing: a modest proposal for a major rethink', IEEE Security & Privacy, 10(2), pp. 24–32.

Kirlappos, I., Parkin, S. and Sasse, M. A., 2015, ''Shadow security' as a tool for the learning organization', ACM SIGCAS Computers and Society, 45(1), pp. 29–37.

Klein, G., 2009, 'Streetlights and shadows: searching for the keys to adaptive decision making'. MIT Press.

Kolb, D. A. and Kolb, A. Y. (quoted in Anderson, E. and Neild, J., 2007), 'Improving self-reflection and peer feedback', Department of Management Working Paper Series, Working Paper 14/07.

Kotter, J. P., 2007, 'Leading change: why transformation efforts fail', Harvard Business Review, 73(2), pp. 1–10.

Kotter, J. P., Akhtar, V. and Gupta, G., 2021, 'Change: how organizations achieve hard-to-imagine results despite uncertain and volatile times'. Wiley, Hoboken, New Jersey.

Kumar, V., Telang, R. and Mukhopadhyay, T., 2007, 'Optimally securing interconnected information systems and assets', Proceedings of the Sixth Workshop on the Economics of Information Security, Carnegie Mellon University, 7–8 June.

Lewin, K., 2013, 'Principles of topological psychology'. Read Books Ltd.

Lovallo, D and Kahneman, D., 2003, 'Delusions of Success: How Optimism Undermines Executives' Decisions', Harvard Business Review.

MacCann, C., Joseph, D. L., Newman, D. A. and Roberts, R. D., 2014, 'Emotional intelligence is a second-stratum factor of intelligence: evidence from hierarchical and bifactor models', Emotion, 14(2), pp. 358–374.

MacLean, P. D., 1990, 'The triune brain in evolution: role in paleocerebral functions'. Springer Science & Business Media.

Maeda, J., 2006, 'The laws of simplicity'. MIT Press.

Maister, D. H., Galford, R. and Green, C., 2021, 'The trusted advisor'. Free Press.

Martins, A. and Eloff, J., 2002, 'Information security culture', Proceedings of the IFIP TC11 17th International Conference on Information Security (SEC2002), Cairo, Egypt, pp. 203–214.

Mayer, J. D., Caruso, D. R. and Salovey, P., 2016, 'The ability model of emotional intelligence: principles and updates', Emotion Review, 8(4), pp. 290–300.

Meadows, D. H., 2008, 'Thinking in systems: a primer'. Chelsea Green Publishing.

Mehrabian, A. and Ferris, S. R., 1967, 'Inference of attitudes from nonverbal communication in two channels', Journal of Consulting Psychology, 31(3), pp. 248–252.

Miao, C., Humphrey, R. H. and Qian, S., 2018, 'A cross-cultural meta-analysis of how leader emotional intelligence influences subordinate task performance and organizational citizenship behavior', Journal of World Business, 53(4), pp. 463–474.

Michie, S., Van Stralen, M. M. and West, R., 2011, 'The behaviour change wheel: a new method for characterising and designing behaviour change interventions', Implementation Science, 6, pp. 1–12.

Mitchell, R. K., Agle, B. R. and Wood, D. J., 1997, 'Toward a theory of stakeholder identification and salience: defining the principle of who and what really counts', Academy of Management Review, 22(4), pp. 853–886.

National Cyber Security Centre (NCSC), 2025, 'Cyber security culture principles'.

Newell, B. R., Lagnado, D. A. and Shanks, D. R., 2022, 'Straight choices: the psychology of decision making'. Psychology Press.

Ngo, L., 2008, 'IT security culture transition process', MSc dissertation, Edith Cowan University, Perth, Australia.

Nicholson, J., Coventry, L. and Briggs, P., 2017, 'Can we fight social engineering attacks by social means? Assessing social salience as a means to improve phish detection', Proceedings of the 13th Symposium on Usable Privacy and Security (SOUPS 2017), Usenix, 12 July, pp. 787–796.

Nielsen, J., 1993, 'Iterative user interface design', IEEE Computer, 26(11), pp. 32–41.

Norman, D. A., 1988, 'The psychology of everyday things'. Basic Books

Norman, D. A., 1993, 'Some observations on mental models', in Gentner, D. A. and Stevens, A. A. (eds.), Mental models, Erlbaum, pp. 206–265.

Ohno, T., 1988, 'Toyota production system: beyond large-scale production'. Productivity Press.

Petitcolas, F. A., 2025, 'Kerckhoffs' principle', Encyclopedia of Cryptography, Security and Privacy, pp. 1342–1343, Cham: Springer Nature Switzerland.

Plattner, H., Meinel, C. and Leifer, L. J. (eds.), 2010, 'Design thinking: understand–improve–apply'. Springer Science & Business Media.

Popper, K. R., 1972, 'Of clocks and clouds: an approach to the problem of rationality and the freedom of man', in Objective knowledge: an evolutionary approach. Clarendon Press, pp. 206–265.

Rasmussen, J., 2012, 'Skills, rules, and knowledge; signals, signs, and symbols, and other distinctions in human performance models', IEEE Transactions on Systems, Man, and Cybernetics, (3), pp. 257–266.

Reason, J., 1990, 'Human error'. Cambridge University Press.

Reis, E., 2011, 'The lean startup'. Crown Business.

Rittel, H. W. J. and Webber, M. M., 1973, 'Dilemmas in a general theory of planning', Policy Sciences, 4, pp. 155–169.

Ross, S. J. and Masters, R., 2011, 'Creating a Culture of Security'. Butterworth-Heinemann

Sasse, M. A., Brostoff, S. and Weirich, D., 2001, 'Transforming the "weakest link": a human–computer interaction approach to usable and effective security', BT Technology Journal, 19(3), pp. 122–131.

Sasse, M. A. and Kirlappos, I., 2014, 'Design for trusted and trustworthy services: why we must do better', Trust, Computing, and Society, pp. 229–249.

Schein, E. H., 1984, 'Coming to a new awareness of organizational culture', Sloan Management Review, 25(2), pp. 3–16.

Schlienger, T. and Teufel, S., 2003, 'Analyzing information security culture: increased trust by an appropriate information security culture', in Proceedings of the 14th International Workshop on Database and Expert Systems Applications, IEEE, pp. 405–409.

Schneier, B., 2000, 'Secrets and lies: digital security in a networked world'. Wiley.

Schneier, B., 2003, 'Beyond Fear: Thinking Sensibly about Security in an Uncertain World'. Copernicus Books, New York.

Schuler, D. and Namioka, A., 1993, 'Participatory design: principles and practices'. CRC Press.

Scott, M. M., 1964, 'Who are your motivated workers?', Harvard Business Review, pp. 73–88.

Shah, P. R., 2024, 'Fogg behavioural model based cybersecurity awareness framework: an empirical analysis', in Indian Conference on Human-Computer Interaction Design and Research, Cham: Springer Nature Switzerland, pp. 51–69.

Sharma, D. N. and Dash, P. K., 2012, 'Effectiveness of ISO 27001 as an information security management system: an analytical study of financial aspects', Far East Journal of Psychology and Business, 9(5), pp. 57–71.

Sherwood, J., Clark, A. and Lynas, D., 2009, 'Enterprise security architecture white paper'.

Shiv, B. and Fedorikhin, A., 1999, 'Heart and mind in conflict: the interplay of affect and cognition in consumer decision making', Journal of Consumer Research, pp. 278–292.

Simon, H. A., 1990, 'Bounded rationality', Utility and Probability, pp. 15–18.

Snowden, D. J. and Boone, M. E., 2007, 'A leader's framework for decision making', Harvard Business Review, 85(11), p. 68.

Son, J.-Y., 2011, 'Out of fear or desire? Toward a better understanding of employees' motivation to follow IS security policies', Information Management, 48(7), pp. 296–302.

Strauss, A. and Corbin, J., 2007, 'Basics of qualitative research: techniques and procedures for developing grounded theory'. Sage Publications Incorporated.

Syed, M., 2015, 'Black box thinking: why most people never learn from their mistakes—but some do'. Penguin.

Taleb, N. N., 2010, 'The black swan: the impact of the highly improbable fragility, Vol. 2'. Random House.

Tanner, B., Cokely, E. T. and Feltz, A., 2025, 'Defaults change choices, not minds: practical and ethical benefits of brief educational boosts for water recycling acceptance', Judgment and Decision Making, 20, p. 30.

Tetlock, P. E. and Gardner, D., 2016, 'Superforecasting: the art and science of prediction'. Random House.

Thaler, R. H. and Sunstein, C. R., 2021, 'Nudge: the final edition'. Penguin.

The European Union Agency for Cybersecurity (ENISA), 2018, 'Cybersecurity culture guidelines: behavioural aspects of cybersecurity'.

Thompson, C. A., Taber, J. M., Sidney, P. G., Fitzsimmons, C. J., Mielicki, M. K., Matthews, P. G., Schemmel, E. A., Simonovic, N., Foust, J. L., Aurora, P. and Disabato, D. J., 2021, 'Math matters: a novel, brief educational intervention decreases whole number bias when reasoning about COVID-19', Journal of Experimental Psychology: Applied, 27(4), p. 632.

Trompeter, C. M. and Eloff, J. H. P., 2001, 'A framework for the implementation of socio-ethical controls in information security', Computers & Security, 20(5), pp. 384–391.

UK Information Commissioner's Office (ICO), 2025, 'Data security incident trends'.

Van Roekel, H., Reinhard, J. and Grimmelikhuijsen, S., 2022, 'Improving hand hygiene in hospitals: comparing the effect of a nudge and a boost on protocol compliance', Behavioural Public Policy, 6(1), pp. 52–74.

Vecchi, G. M., Van Hasselt, V. B. and Romano, S. J., 2005, 'Crisis (hostage) negotiation: current strategies and issues in high-risk conflict resolution', Aggression and Violent Behavior, 10(5), pp. 533–551.

Von Solms, B. and Von Solms, R., 2005, 'From information security to business security', Computers & Security, 24(4), pp. 271–273.

Vroom, C. and Von Solms, R., 2004, 'Towards information security behavioural compliance', Computers & Security, 23(3), pp. 191–198.

Walter, F., Cole, M. S. and Humphrey, R. H., 2011, 'Emotional intelligence: sine qua non of leadership or folderol?', Academy of Management Perspectives, 25(1), pp. 45–59.

Wang, Y., Leon, P. G., Acquisti, A., Cranor, L. F., Forget, A. and Sadeh, N., 2014, 'A field trial of privacy nudges for Facebook', Proceedings of the 32nd Annual ACM Conference on Human Factors in Computing Systems (CHI '14), New York, NY, USA, pp. 2367–2376.

Wash, R., 2010, 'Folk models of home computer security', Proceedings of the Sixth Symposium on Usable Privacy and Security, ACM.

Weber, M., 1978, 'Economy and society: an outline of interpretive sociology, Vol. 1'. University of California Press.

Weirich, D. and Sasse, M. A., 2001, 'Pretty good persuasion: a first step towards effective password security for the real world', Proceedings of the New Security Paradigms Workshop, Cloudcroft, NM: ACM Press, pp. 137–143.

Whitten, A. and Tygar, J. D., 1999, 'Why Johnny can't encrypt: a usability evaluation of PGP 5.0',

Proceedings of the 8th USENIX Security Symposium, Washington, DC, August, pp. 169–184.

Williams, E. J., Beardmore, A. and Joinson, A. N., 2017, 'Individual differences in susceptibility to online influence: a theoretical review', Computers in Human Behavior, 72, pp. 412–421.

Wilson, J. Q. and Kelling, G. L., 1982, 'Broken windows: the police and neighborhood safety', The Atlantic, 29(31), pp. 29–38.

Wilson, T., 2004, 'Strangers to ourselves', Harvard University Press.

Witte, K. and Allen, M., 2000, 'A meta-analysis of fear appeals: implications for effective public health programs', Health Education and Behavior, 27(5), pp. 591–615.

Wood, C. C., 2000, 'An unappreciated reason why information security policies fail', Computer Fraud & Security, 10, pp. 13–14.

Wood, R. E., 1986, 'Task complexity: definition of the construct', Organizational Behavior and Human Decision Processes, 37(1), pp. 60–82.

Woods, D., Dekker, S., Cook, R., Johannesen, L. and Sarter, N., 2017, 'Behind human error'. CRC Press.

Yee, K. P., 2005, 'User interaction design for secure systems', in Cranor, L. F. and Garfinkel, S. (eds.), Security and usability: designing secure systems that people can use. O'Reilly Books, pp. 13–30.

Yukl, G., Seifert, C. F. and Chavez, C., 2008, 'Validation of the extended influence behavior questionnaire', The Leadership Quarterly, 19(5), pp. 609–621.

Zinatullin, L., 2013, 'Modelling conflicts between security compliance and human behaviour', dissertation, University College London.

Zurko, M. E. and Simon, R. T., 1996, 'User-centred security', Proceedings of the 1996 Workshop on New Security Paradigms, pp. 27–33.

FURTHER READING

GRC Solutions is the world's leading publisher for governance and compliance. Our industry-leading pocket guides, books and training resources are written by real-world practitioners and thought leaders. They are used globally by audiences of all levels, from students to C-suite executives.

Our high-quality publications cover all IT governance, risk and compliance frameworks and are available in a range of formats. This ensures our customers can access the information they need in the way they need it.

Other books you may find useful include:

- Managing AI Risk: A practical approach to responsibly managing AI with ISO 42001 by Andrew Pattison *https://www.itgovernance.co.uk/shop/product/managing-ai-risk-a-practical-approach-to-responsibly-managing-ai-with-iso-42001*
- Digital Ethics in the Age of AI – Navigating the ethical frontier today and beyond by Dr Julie E. Mehan *https://www.itgovernance.co.uk/shop/product/digital-ethics-in-the-age-of-ai-navigating-the-ethical-frontier-today-and-beyond*
- ISO 27001/ISO 27002 - A guide to information security management systems by Alan Calder *ISO 27001/ISO 27002 – An introduction to information security standards | IT Governance UK*

For more information on GRC Solutions and IT Governance™, a GRC Solutions Company as well as branded publishing services, please visit *https://www.itgovernance.co.uk/*.

Branded publishing

Through our branded publishing service, you can customise our publications with your organisation's branding. For more information, please contact *clientservices-uk@grcsolutions.io*.

Related services

GRC Solutions offers a comprehensive range of complementary products and services to help organisations meet their objectives.

For a full range of resources, please visit *www.itgovernance.co.uk*.

Training services

GRC Solutions' training programme is built on our extensive practical experience designing and implementing management systems based on ISO standards, best practice and regulations.

Our courses help attendees develop practical skills and comply with contractual and regulatory requirements. They also support career development via recognised qualifications.

Learn more about our training courses and view the full course catalogue at *www.itgovernance.co.uk/training*.

Professional services and consultancy

We are a leading global consultancy of IT governance, risk management and compliance solutions. We advise organisations around the world on their most critical issues and present cost-saving and risk-reducing solutions based on international best practice and frameworks.

We offer a wide range of delivery methods to suit all budgets, timescales and preferred project approaches.

Find out how our consultancy services can help your organisation at *www.itgovernance.co.uk/consulting*.

Industry news

Want to stay up to date with the latest developments and resources in the IT governance and compliance market? Subscribe to our Security Spotlight newsletter and we will send you mobile-friendly emails with fresh news and features about your preferred areas of interest, as well as unmissable offers and free resources to help you successfully start your project:

www.itgovernance.co.uk/security-spotlight-newsletter.

EU for product safety is Stephen Evans, The Mill Enterprise Hub, Stagreenan,
Drogheda, Co. Louth, A92 CD3D, Ireland. (servicecentre@itgovernance.eu)

www.ingramcontent.com/pod-product-compliance
Ingram Content Group UK Ltd.
Pitfield, Milton Keynes, MK11 3LW, UK
UKHW050210110226
10625UKWH00010B/178
* 9 7 8 1 7 8 7 7 8 6 0 9 7 *